HIV & AIDS

The Essential Guide

Jennifer
Reinoehl

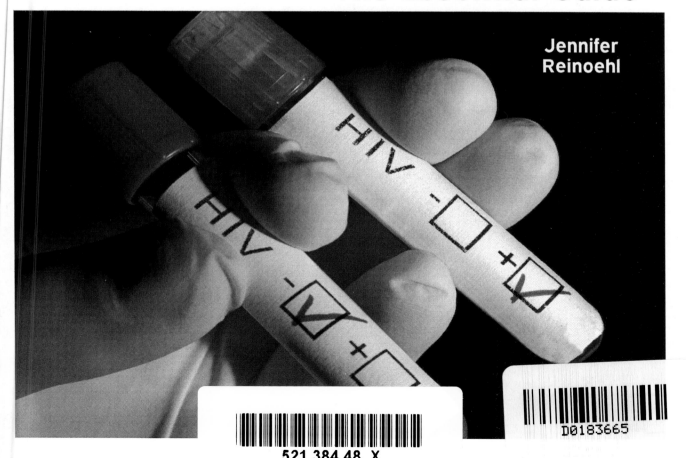

HIV & AIDS: The Essential Guide is also available in accessible formats for people with any degree of visual impairment. The large print edition and e-book (with accessibility features enabled) are available from Need2Know. Please let us know if there are any special features you require and we will do our best to accommodate your needs.

First published in Great Britain in 2013 by
Need2Know
Remus House
Coltsfoot Drive
Peterborough
PE2 9BF
Telephone 01733 898103
Fax 01733 313524
www.need2knowbooks.co.uk

Contents

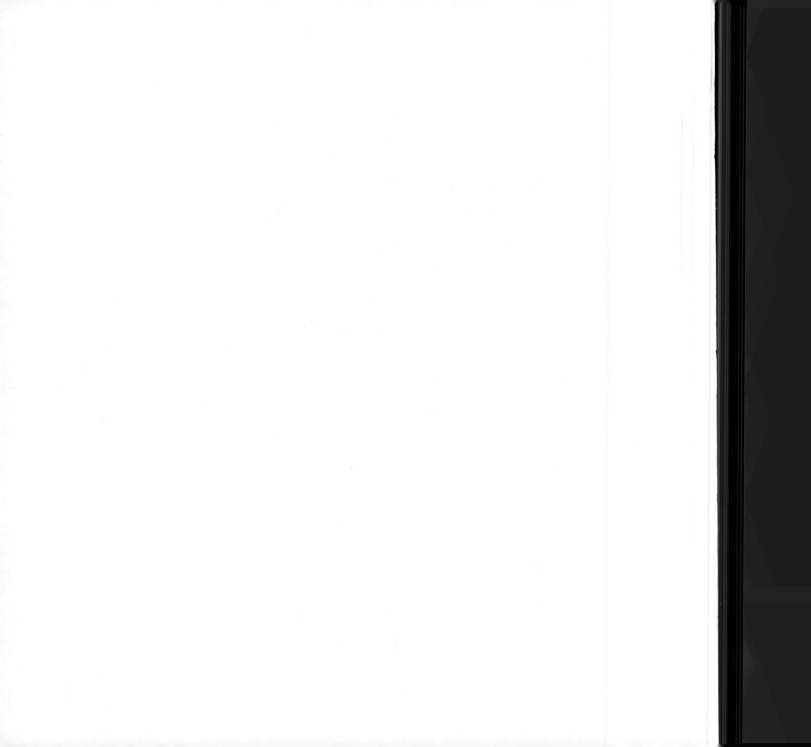

Introduction

HIV is spreading across the United Kingdom at a disturbing rate. It causes lowered immunity, an increased risk for cancer, flu-like symptoms, and death. The weakened immune system not only increases susceptibility to common diseases, but also allows the body to become sick with diseases healthy people never develop. HIV is transmitted through fluids produced by the body. Common ways people contract HIV are through donated blood, men who have sex with men, and intravenous drug use. It is estimated more than 90,000 Britons carry HIV, and the number increases each year.

While the medical profession is finding new drugs to keep HIV-positive patients alive, the best method for surviving HIV and AIDS is never to acquire it in the first place. Not only do people who have AIDS require intensive drug therapy, they frequently become so sick that they can no longer work. Although modern drug therapies have been able to delay the onset of AIDS, it is important for early diagnosis and monitoring for the best chances of success.

HIV is difficult to diagnose in its earliest stages because its symptoms are similar to those of the flu. To make matters even more difficult, the HIV test may give a false negative if taken too soon after infection. When the initial symptoms subside it can take years for HIV to re-emerge and devastate the immune system. During this time, HIV-positive individuals may go on to infect many other people unknowingly. Two-thirds of the people who died with HIV in 2010 had been first diagnosed when the disease had progressed too far for effective antiretroviral treatment.

If you have been diagnosed with HIV or AIDS, you may be confused or feel powerless. You may be experiencing symptoms, side effects, or you may have just discovered that you carry the disease. Although there is currently no cure for HIV, it is important to understand your condition, so you can continue to live your life to its fullest. It is also important to understand the side effects you may have from your treatment and the importance of working through them with your doctor so you can continue on your drug therapy. Staying healthy and following the instructions of your healthcare provider can help you live longer and perhaps be available for more efficient treatments of the future.

'It is estimated more than 90,000 Britons carry HIV, and the number increases each year.'

HIV is not a condition that only affects homosexuals or men or Africans. HIV affects the young and the old, the homeless drug user and the rich businessman. This book is written for anyone who has been diagnosed with HIV, their loved ones, and their friends. It has the most recent information on HIV and AIDS. It will inform you on what the disease is, what current treatments are available, how the treatments work, what new developments are just around the corner, and how to avoid risks of contracting the disease. It is written to explain in detail the things you have heard from your healthcare professional. People who are informed about HIV and who know how to manage the disease successfully, regain some power over their future outcome.

Disclaimer

'HIV affects the young and the old, the homeless drug user and the rich businessman.'

This book is a source of general information on HIV and AIDS, and it is not intended to replace the advice of a healthcare professional. It is crucial to obtain professional medical advice if you are HIV-positive, or think you may be HIV-positive, in order to receive a proper diagnosis. At the time of going to press, all of the information in this edition was accurate. However, national recommendations and guidelines can change at any time.

Chapter One

What Is HIV and AIDS?

Definition and overview

HIV

HIV is the acronym for 'human immunodeficiency virus'. It uses the word 'human' because although the disease may have originally been transmitted to humans through monkeys, it currently is transmitted from human to human. 'Immunodeficiency' means that the disease attacks the immune system and weakens it. A 'virus' is an infectious particle that requires a living cell in order to make copies of it. HIV is a virus that attacks the human immune system. Once it finds a way into your body it searches the bloodstream for certain cells of the immune system. It then enters the cells and uses them to reproduce. This causes your cells to either commit suicide, be killed by the other parts of your immune system once the infection is recognised, or die from working too hard for the HIV. With fewer cells available to fight off other infections, your body is unable to cope with even the simplest diseases.

'HIV is a virus that attacks the human immune system.'

HIV was first detected in blood samples stored from 1959. A man from Kinshasa, Democratic Republic of Congo is the first known human carrier. In that same year, David Carr died with it in Manchester. At the time, these deaths were mysterious, but not considered related. Evidence of a new disease was not collected until the mid-1970s.

In the early 1980s, doctors began to realise there was a growing problem among gay men that was associated with an unknown syndrome. These healthy men were suddenly contracting rare diseases that only people with weak immune systems got. Then they were mysteriously dying. The only thing they all seemed to have in common was that they had numerous, unknown sexual partners. Some other patterns, such as having STIs, also began to emerge. However, the disease was only affecting the homosexual community and some illegal drug users. The new disease was named GRID (gay-related immunodeficiency).

After a couple more years, it was discovered that the men who died from GRID were all infected with a newly discovered virus termed 'HIV.' When children and heterosexual people began to catch HIV and develop symptoms of this mysterious syndrome, the original name 'GRID' was changed to 'AIDS'.

AIDS

'While HIV is the name given to the virus, AIDS is the name given to the disease. You can be infected with HIV without having AIDS.'

AIDS is the acronym for 'acquired immune deficiency syndrome'. 'Acquired' means that it is given from one person to the next through body fluids. In other words, it is not inherited. Like HIV, its acronym tells us that the disease affects the immune system. 'Syndrome' is for the group of symptoms that form a pattern. This pattern is what early doctors were able to recognise as unique to this disease in order to make the diagnosis. Once HIV advances to AIDS, people begin to develop rare diseases that kill them. No matter what people call it, AIDS has long been a disease that mystifies even the most experienced and astute doctors.

While HIV is the name given to the virus, AIDS is the name given to the disease. You can be infected with HIV without having AIDS. With most viruses, there is a standard incubation period or a standard amount of time from when you take the virus into your body until the virus gives you identifying symptoms of the disease. However, with HIV and AIDS, the time for HIV to become AIDS is different from individual to individual. Instead of an incubation period, HIV is said to have a window. The HIV window is measured from the time when a person is first infected with the disease to the time the infection can be detected with a standard ELISA test (see chapter 3). This time is 1-6 months.

Because people with HIV tend not to have symptoms of the disease during the first stage of the infection, it is called the acute stage of infection. Although a person who has been infected can get positive results in as little as four weeks, lack of symptoms means it is often years before a person is diagnosed.

Although some people who contract HIV will develop flu-like symptoms within four weeks, an individual is only diagnosed with AIDS after he or she begins to develop other rare diseases. It is only after the immune system begins to fail due to the HIV that a person is considered to have AIDS. AIDS can take up to ten years to develop from the time a person initially contracted HIV.

What is a virus?

A virus consists of genetic material surrounded by a protein covering. It infects cells and uses them to reproduce. Unlike bacteria and parasites, which are living organisms that perform chemical changes inside them in order to make energy and break down nutrients, viruses cannot do anything by themselves. They do not need energy to survive, and they steal the energy and nutrients made by your cells to reproduce.

Because viruses do not operate on their own, they do not have the complex structure that is found inside cells. If you think about your body, you know it has different parts – for example, a heart, a brain and a stomach. Each cell in your body has similar parts. A virus has only an outside cover, an inside cover and genetic material (directions). Sometimes they also have a few small tools with them, but they cannot use the tools without stealing energy from a living cell. If a virus were as big as a body, it would only have two layers of skin and a brain and maybe a few blood cells.

The outside layer of a virus is called a protein coat. This part of the virus finds and locks onto the cell it will infect. Once it has locked on, the cell will let the virus into it, and the virus can begin to use the cell to make more copies of it. Some viruses kill the cells they infect by making so many copies the cells explode, other viruses just work the cells to death. Some viruses, like the chickenpox (varicella zoster) virus, will hibernate inside cells. These do not begin making copies of themselves again unless something happens to lower the defense of your immune system. HIV is another virus that goes into hibernation after its initial attack on your immune system, but it is uncertain what causes it to re-emerge.

'It is only after the immune system begins to fail due to the HIV that a person is considered to have AIDS. AIDS can take up to ten years to develop from the time a person initially contracted HIV.'

Viruses are classified into seven different categories depending on what they are made out of and how they reproduce. Because viruses are so simple, they are made primarily from genetic material. DNA (deoxyribonucleic acid) and RNA (ribonucleic acid) are the genetic materials that contain genes, which are the directions that tell cells what to do.

Viruses can be made from DNA or RNA. They can be one strand of the material, or they can be two strands. Most viruses, whether they are made from DNA or RNA, enter a cell and begin reproducing immediately. Retroviruses, such as HIV, actually must go against the normal life process and make DNA out of their RNA before they are able to reproduce.

Who is likely to develop HIV/AIDS?

There are people at high risk for becoming infected with HIV, who engage in behaviours that increase their risk. These people, for whatever reason, do not take personal precautions to prevent themselves from either being infected or from passing the infection on to others. There are other people who are also at risk, but they are not actively or deliberately engaging in behaviours that are risky. They may be just as unaware as those engaging in risky behaviours, but they could receive the virus only through passive means.

High-risk people, or people who are doing things that put themselves at greater risk for catching HIV are:

- People who have unprotected sex.
- People who share needles, rinse water, syringes or other injection equipment.
- People who receive tattoos or piercings from parlours that do not look after their equipment in a way that prevents cross-contamination.
- Sexually active people carrying other sexually transmitted infections.
- People who have open and uncovered sores or wounds.

People who are at risk for catching HIV and who are not deliberately doing anything that would put themselves at high risk are:

- Babies of HIV mothers who have not received treatment for the disease.

- Healthcare workers.
- Patients who have received blood transfusions (blood, platelets or plasma transferred from one person to another person who needs it).
- Patients who have received organ transplants.
- People who are injured by needles outside of a healthcare situation.

What is the difference between HIV and AIDS?

HIV is the name of the virus that initially attacks the body. A person is usually diagnosed as being HIV-positive when the body responds to the initial attack by producing antibodies to fight HIV. Antibodies are proteins made by your immune system to capture diseases and help break them down. This response can occur in as little as four weeks, and once it occurs the person will test positive for HIV.

Initially, the virus battles with the immune system and is beaten into hiding somewhere in the body. At some point, it will come back en masse and overwhelm the immune system. When it does this, other rare diseases are able to attack the body. Under normal conditions, a healthy person may not have any symptoms of these opportunistic infections because the immune system destroys them quickly. However, a person who has a compromised immune system will not be able to fight the diseases because it will be losing its soldiers in its battle with HIV. When a person has been diagnosed as being HIV-positive and he or she has contracted one of these rare opportunistic infections, he or she is considered to have AIDS.

What is the difference between HIV-1 and HIV-2?

The HIV virus is very small. It contains only nine genes that make 19 different proteins. Although all HIV can cause AIDS, these genes are slightly changing or mutating each time it makes copies. It constantly changes because it reproduces quickly but not carefully. In addition, when two different HIVs meet

'HIV is the name of the virus that initially attacks the body. A person is usually diagnosed as being HIV-positive when the body responds to the initial attack by producing antibodies to fight HIV.'

inside the same cell, they can exchange some of their genes with each other. For this reason, there can be a big difference between the drugs one person with HIV uses to keep it under control and the drugs another person uses.

Researchers like to break the HIV down into different groups to help treat each subgroup more effectively. The largest split they have identified divides HIV into two different types: HIV-1 and HIV-2. Both of these forms of HIV cause AIDS, but HIV-2 seems to be more difficult to pass from one person to the next. In addition, the time it takes for HIV-2 to turn into AIDS is longer than the time it takes for HIV-1 to follow the same process. When scientists look at the virus on a genetic level, HIV-1 is closely related to the highly infective SIVcpz (a chimpanzee form of HIV). HIV-2 is more closely related to SIVsmm (a sooty mangabey form of HIV).

Because HIV-2 is a less deadly form of the virus that is found mainly in West Africa, it is rarely the focus of most research. When people talk about HIV without adding the type, they are referring to HIV-1. HIV-1 has more mutated forms than HIV-2, it attacks quicker and mutates faster that HIV-2, and it is more difficult to treat because of the many combinations of drug resistance it can develop.

Drug resistance occurs when a disease stops responding to a medicine because something in the disease directions changed. For example, assume one medicine works by attaching to a tool and preventing it from doing its job. If the shape of the tool changes so that the medicine can no longer attach to it, the medicine will stop working.

When HIV-1 is classified into its different groups, the classification is based on the drugs to which it is resistant. An example of some of the groups, are the M, N, and O groups. Each of these specific groups has a slightly different form of the gene that makes the outside coating of the virus. Because the outside coating determines if the HIV can bind to the T-cell, the medicines that interfere with this binding are affected by these particular mutations. Healthcare providers will usually test a person with HIV before he or she is placed on medications to determine which mutations of the HIV are present and to which drugs the HIV will not respond well.

'HIV-1 has more mutated forms than HIV-2, it attacks quicker and mutates faster that HIV-2, and it is more difficult to treat because of the many combinations of drug resistance it can develop.'

What is a T-cell?

Inside blood, there are red blood cells that give blood its colour, white blood cells that help fight infection and platelets that help your body form scabs when you are injured. Although platelets and red blood cells have one basic form, there are many different types of white blood cells.

All white blood cells, such as B-lymphocytes and T-lymphocytes, help fight infection in different ways. Some make antigens, which imprison infectious particles; others eat imprisoned particles and break them into pieces so they can no longer function.

One type of white blood cell is a T-cell. T-cells actually have several names. Sometimes they are called CD4 cells, CD4+ T-cells, helper T-cells, or even CD4 T-lymphocytes. CD4 is a binding protein (a key-like finger made from protein) on the outside of the T-cell that allows the HIV to grab on to it.

When T-cells are working, they help other white blood cells to break apart infectious particles, and they help B-lymphocytes reproduce. When the number of T-cells is low, the entire immune system struggles to work.

'When the number of T-cells is low, the entire immune system struggles to work.'

What is happening inside my body when I have HIV?

HIV is made from RNA, which is a string of genes slightly different from the DNA that controls your cells. When HIV gets into your body, it attaches to a T-cell. When it attaches, it unlocks the door to get inside the T-cell. Once HIV is inside the cell, it uses some of the cell's energy to make a copy of itself in DNA. As DNA, it can sneak into the cell's control center (nucleus) and attach itself to your cell's DNA. The cell cannot tell the difference between its own information and the virus information.

The virus then tells the cell to make millions of copies of it. The cell obeys but eventually uses all its energy and nutrients making the copies. This causes the cell to die.

At first, the HIV levels in your body rise rapidly, but your immune system realises what is happening and tries to fight against it with antibodies. The antibodies imprison the virus and help break it into pieces so it will no longer work. At this point, a HIV test will come back positive.

As soon as your body fights back, the HIV decides to hide inside cells in your body. When the HIV is outside the T-cells floating around, the HIV can be captured and imprisoned by antibodies. Inside your cells, it is safe. Because the standard HIV test looks for antibodies, you will still test positive, but you will have very little or no detectable HIV in your blood. Some virus is still being produced and released, however, the HIV is just not working at full capacity.

Then, for reasons unknown, the HIV will suddenly begin to make many copies of itself again. It copies itself so much that it begins to destroy most of your T-cells. After that, your body begins having trouble fighting any infections, even the ones that did not previously make you sick. Opportunistic infections appear, and AIDS is diagnosed.

'There is no cure for HIV or AIDS.'

Is HIV/AIDS a serious condition?

When HIV was first discovered in the early 1980s, the time it took for HIV to display the symptoms of AIDS was less than ten years. A HIV-positive person would die within five years after the AIDS diagnosis.

As new drugs developed in the 1990s and drug therapies included combination drugs, the time it took for HIV to display the symptoms of AIDS grew longer. Now there are highly effective drugs even for the opportunistic infections that occur. All of these factors contribute to an overall public feeling that AIDS is no longer such a threat.

However, there is no cure for HIV or AIDS. At this time, HIV has almost a 100% death rate, which gives it a higher death rate than the Plague of the 1600s. Although it is not a swift killer, it should still be taken very seriously. Only people who discover they have the disease quickly and seek immediate treatment will live a full life. Those who have the disease and ignore or deny it, risk spreading it to others and dying sooner. Globally, every five seconds a new person is infected with the AIDS virus, and every year three million people die from it or conditions caused by it.

Get tested, and if you practise risky behaviours, get tested frequently. If you are diagnosed with HIV, find a healthcare professional that you trust. Be sure that he or she has experience with HIV and AIDS. Begin to work out a plan for monitoring the disease and for treating it. Once your doctor provides you with a treatment plan, be sure to follow it. Also, make lifestyle changes that will keep you healthy.

'Globally, every five seconds a new person is infected with the AIDS virus, and every year three million people die from it or conditions caused by it.'

Summing Up

- HIV is a disease that affects the immune system of humans. At first, it struck isolated locations around the world, but then it became increasingly prevalent. Originally, it was also thought to affect only gay men, but soon case numbers among all populations grew.

- A virus is a small particle that consists of genetic material surrounded by a protein covering. It infects cells and uses them to reproduce.

- People who practise risky behaviours, such as having unprotected sex with multiple partners and sharing needles during drug use, are more likely to catch HIV. Some people can passively be exposed, such as babies of HIV-positive women and transplant recipients.

- HIV is the virus that infects people. AIDS is the disease that appears when that virus takes over the immune system.

- HIV-1 and HIV-2 are two different types of HIV. Both can become AIDS. HIV-1 is the most predominant form of HIV, and that is the form people are talking about if they only say HIV.

- T-cells are cells of the immune system that can become infected with HIV. They are also known as CD4 T-lymphocytes.

- HIV takes over the cells of your immune system and forces them to make more HIVs. This process kills the cells of your immune system and makes your body more susceptible to other diseases.

- HIV is an extremely serious condition. People who exhibit risky behaviours should be tested even if they do not have symptoms of AIDS. People who are found to be HIV-positive should seek the advice and care of an experienced physician as soon as possible.

Chapter Two

How Can You Contract HIV and AIDS?

What are the symptoms?

During the first stage of HIV infection, or what is also known as the acute stage, you may feel mild, flu-like symptoms. Fever, headache, fatigue, rashes, diarrhoea, swollen lymph nodes and muscle aches are symptoms that could signal a HIV infection or several other diseases. These symptoms can occur anywhere from 2-8 weeks after you become infected. They are the result of your body attempting to fight the disease. When the disease hides, you will probably feel fine again and forget you even had these initial symptoms.

Even when the virus is hidden, it can still produce up to one trillion more HIVs in a day. As the HIV levels begin to rise in your system, you may begin to feel unwell again. You could develop another skin rash and have continued fatigue, but you also may lose a little weight. A yeast infection in your mouth, called 'thrush' could develop, and you might experience night sweats. Women might start noticing some irregularities in their periods, vaginal and yeast infections that keep on coming back, and they may have herpes, human papillomavirus (HPV), or pelvic inflammatory disease (PID) outbreaks. Although herpes causes uncomfortable ulcers, it is relatively common among people with and without HIV. HPV causes genital warts, which may be a little more concerning, but not everybody who is infected with HPV gets warts. PID affects only women and can be without symptoms or it can cause fever, lower abdominal pain or pain during intercourse, changes in vaginal discharge and menstruation irregularities. Most people are still not worried at this point and might not suspect they are infected.

'Fever, headache, fatigue, rashes, diarrhoea, swollen lymph nodes and muscle aches are symptoms that could signal a HIV infection.'

It can take up to ten years before HIV causes a major drop in the number of T-cells in your body. The HIV concentrations in your blood increase during this time. If the T-cells are measured here they would have dropped from between 500-1,800 per mm^3 to below 500 per mm^3. An opportunistic infection usually will appear as soon as your CD4 count drops below 500 cells/mm^3, which will alert a doctor to the possibility of AIDS. It is during this third stage that a person is usually diagnosed with AIDS. The diagnosis requires a blood test that shows the person is HIV-positive and a confirmation of one of the opportunistic infections associated with HIV.

False and exaggerated rumours about how HIV/AIDS is spread

'In a recent study performed by the National AIDS Trust, it was discovered that only 30% of the people could correctly identify all the ways that AIDS can and cannot be spread.'

It is very difficult to not listen to the rumors that people spread about HIV. On the surface, many of them seem to make sense. In a recent study performed by the National AIDS Trust, it was discovered that only 30% of the people could correctly identify all the ways that AIDS can and cannot be spread. Remember to trust your healthcare provider to answer any questions about rumors that you hear. Here are just a few:

- You can get HIV from insect bites – This rumour is easy to believe. After all, who has not heard about the diseases, such as malaria and yellow fever, which insects carry? To answer this rumour, think about the common cold. No one has yet complained that a fly bit them and gave them a cold. Why not? Mosquitoes do not carry the cold from one person to the next. Malaria happens to be one of the rare diseases that does live inside a mosquito. Neither the common cold nor HIV can do that. An insect transmits diseases through its saliva, and HIV is not found in insect saliva. It may also add a little reassurance to know that once a mosquito bites a person, it will not immediately fly to someone else and bite him or her. Any blood or disease-causing agents left on the insect's mouth will be gone before it decides to feed again.

- You can get HIV if an infected person coughs or sneezes on you – Some diseases are transmitted through the air, but HIV is thankfully not transmitted this way. You may get a cold or perhaps the flu if someone sneezes and coughs on you, but this could happen whether you are HIV-positive or not.

- You can get HIV by kissing an infected person – There is really no way to be exposed to HIV if you are kissing with your mouth closed. If you are kissing with an open mouth, there is a very slight chance of becoming infected. If both the uninfected person and the infected person have cuts or bleeding gums, the saliva could allow enough of the HIV to enter the uninfected person's bloodstream and infect him or her. However, saliva has properties that block HIV so the infected person would have to have an extraordinarily heavy viral load. There has never been a known incident of one person contracting HIV from another person by just kissing them.

- You can get HIV if an infected person bites you and breaks the skin – Four people in the entire history of the disease have gotten HIV after being bitten, so the chances of becoming infected this way are very slim. In order for HIV to be transmitted, there would have to be enough damage to have drawn blood. If the infected person were biting you, he or she would need to have a heavy viral load and open, bleeding mouth sores. If another person ever bites you, it is always a good idea to seek immediate medical attention. If you are the person doing the biting, you have open mouth sores, and you get a mouthful of blood, you could get infected if the other person has HIV.

- You can get HIV if an infected individual scratches you – This is false. HIV lives in body fluids. In order to be exposed to HIV, you need to allow an infected person's body fluids into your body. Scratching does not provide that exchange.

- You can get HIV if a HIV-positive person spits on you or if you share a glass with him or her – There has never been a documented case of this happening. HIV can be present in the person's spit, but saliva has the power to render it inactive, especially when in small amounts. HIV also needs to have a way into your body. HIV cannot pass through unbroken skin, and it does not live long in spit or on dry surfaces.

- You can get HIV by sharing the same toilet as a person who is positive – HIV is not secreted through the skin, and it does not live on toilet seats. HIV needs a liquid like human blood or semen to live.

- You can get HIV if a needle pricks you – Again, there have been *no documented cases* of a needle prick transmitting HIV outside of a healthcare situation. If, however, you are cleaning up used needles or other injection devices, and you are pricked, get immediate medical attention. You can

'There have been *no documented cases* of a needle prick transmitting HIV outside of a healthcare situation.'

receive a post-exposure prophylaxis (PEP) to prevent infection. PEP treatments need to begin within 72 hours of exposure. You will need to continue them for one month.

- You can catch HIV if you play football with someone who has it – There have been several professional sports players who have contracted AIDS, but none of them contracted the disease on the playing field. Some games, like rugby or boxing, are a little more violent and prone to drawing blood. When a player is injured, the game should be stopped and the injury cleaned and bandaged before it resumes. By immediately caring for all open wounds, it will prevent any disease being transmitted. It will also reduce the chances of the wound becoming infected.

'The only way hospitals contributed to the spread of HIV occurred in the days before testing was done on donated organs and blood.'

Do drugs users have an increased risk for contracting HIV/AIDS?

People who use drugs casually or people who are addicted to them both have an increased chance of developing HIV. A person using drugs is more likely to practise the risky behaviour of sharing injection needles. When more than one person uses one needle, each person leaves a bit of his or her blood in it. When blood from an infected person is allowed into an uninfected person's body, HIV can spread. There is also an added risk for a drug user because they are more likely to practise unprotected sex when they are under the influence of drugs.

Can I get HIV/AIDS from hospital?

Most hospitals do not allow one patient's blood or bodily fluid to mingle with another person's blood. Without an exchange of fluids, there can be no transmission of HIV. The only way hospitals contributed to the spread of HIV occurred in the days before testing was done on donated organs and blood. Several people, who received transfusions or donated organs when AIDS was first discovered, contracted HIV from them. In recent years, methods of effectively testing tissue and organ donors have cleansed the supply. Third World countries that are still developing may not be able to provide the same level of prevention. Worldwide, the World Health Organization (WHO) estimates that 5%-10% of all HIV cases came from infected blood transfusions. These now occur only in underdeveloped countries.

How do I avoid contracting HIV/AIDS?

The best way to avoid catching HIV is to play it safe:

- Always assume another person may have HIV and thus limit your contact with other people's blood and *never* have unprotected sex with anyone whose sexual history you are not certain of, or anyone you don't 100% know is HIV-negative.

- Abstinence is 100% effective against the transmission of any sexually transmitted disease. (Abstinence means no oral, anal or vaginal sex.) Monogamy is also very safe as long as you and your partner have both been tested.

- Learn how to use a condom effectively. Always put the condom on when the male is erect. Always withdraw and remove the condom immediately after the male ejaculates. Studies have shown that condoms are 90% effective in preventing AIDS transmission.

- Never use a lambskin condom, they do not protect from HIV. Polyurethane condoms are more likely to break. Nonoxynol-9 will break down latex condoms. Use only water-soluble lubrication with condoms.

- Keep condoms in a dry, cool place and do not use them if they are damaged or ripped. Never reuse a condom, and never share a used condom with another individual.

- All the rules for male condoms also apply to female condoms, except female condoms can be inserted up to eight hours in advanced of sexual activity.

- Use a condom if you perform oral sex on men and use a dental dam with the starch rinsed from it or some plastic wrap for oral sex on women.

- Use condoms on sex toys you share.

- Do not share any drug paraphernalia.

- Never handle any used needles/syringes without taking the necessary precautions and using the correct safety equipment, to avoid needle pricks.

- There is extensive evidence that circumcised males are less likely to contract and spread HIV. However, if you are an uncircumcised adult, always discuss the risks and benefits of the procedure before deciding whether to have it performed.

Is there a vaccine?

HIV is extremely variable. Vaccines work by teaching your body what a virus looks like. The body can then make antibodies in advance of infection that will immediately imprison that infection. For years, people have been trying to devise a vaccine for AIDS, but they keep having difficulty with the fact that HIV has many varieties. We discussed the two different types of HIV in chapter 1. Within the HIV-1 type the M group alone has nine more subtypes. Each variation would require a different vaccine so your body could recognise it and destroy it before it attacked. Needless to say, finding a way for the body to recognise and defend against all the different forms of HIV has proved to be challenging.

There is something called a therapeutic HIV vaccine that is currently being developed. This is for people who have already been diagnosed as HIV-positive. Unlike vaccines that prevent disease, these vaccines are not designed to help the immune system fight HIV without drugs. They were created as an optional way of extending HIV treatment.

For people who are not infected, modern AIDS medications have recently worked to stop the spread of AIDS. Pre-exposure prophylaxis (PrEP) is giving a person who is HIV-negative ART medications before they are exposed to HIV. This could be used for couples who are sero-discordant (one is HIV-positive and the other is HIV-negative) and who want to have a child together naturally. PrEP has the potential to be used as a general preventative if the HIV-negative person in a relationship can live with the side effects for the long term. If PrEP becomes a general preventative, it should be used with condoms to increase its effectiveness. PrEP could also be used in special circumstances where, for instance, a person wanted to get a tattoo, but was unsure of the needle safety.

The possible adverse qualities of PrEP are that a HIV-negative person may feel they are safe taking the ART, but contract a form of HIV that is resistant to the ART they use. It is also uncertain what the long-term effects of taking ART will be on future strains of HIV and its drug resistance.

Post-exposure prophylaxis (PEP) is using ART to prevent HIV transmission after a HIV-negative person has been exposed to HIV. PEP has been used to successfully prevent the transmission of HIV if you begin treatment within 72 hours after exposure. If you have been exposed to HIV recently or are considering future plans that may expose you, talk to your doctor to see if either of the treatments will work to meet your needs.

The vicious cycle of HIV/AIDS transmission

When a person contracts HIV, it can go undetected for an entire decade. Even if the person gets sick right away, they may not have built any antibodies for the tests to measure. The sickness may be mild enough to ignore. The earliest a blood test can be performed is within 2-8 weeks of contracting the disease. If this initial test is negative, a second test should be performed in 3-6 months. Without this diligence, a person can go for years without realising they are carrying a deadly disease around with them. During this time, it is still possible for them to infect others even if they do not develop any symptoms of AIDS. When the others are infected, the cycle begins again. It is important to be tested every year for HIV if you are doing any of the following risky behaviours:

- Injecting illegal drugs or sharing any injection materials with other people (including insulin needles).

- Exchanging sex for money, drugs, or other things.

- Have sex with multiple partners or with a partner who has had multiple partners.

- If you were recently treated for tuberculosis, a sexually transmitted infections, or hepatitis.

- Are having sex with someone who has done one or more of these behaviours.

'PEP has been used to successfully prevent the transmission of HIV if you begin treatment within 72 hours after exposure.'

Summing Up

- The initial symptoms of HIV are like the flu. These may go away and come back, or you may develop a rash on your skin, weight loss and a yeast infection in your mouth. When your body succumbs to HIV and it turns into AIDS, you can develop opportunistic infections and have the symptoms of those.

- Rumours may sound true enough and some may even have a little bit of fact to back them, but most have no basis in truth. Talk any questions you have about contracting HIV over with your doctor.

- Drug use is a risky behaviour. Not only can you catch HIV from sharing needles, but you can also get it from engaging in unprotected sex while under the influence of drugs.

- You can only get HIV from a hospital if you receive a transfusion or organ transplant that has not been tested for HIV. Hospitals in the United Kingdom do an excellent job of keeping their patients safe from HIV contamination through their rigorous testing procedure.

- To reduce your risks for HIV infection, protect yourself by using a condom barrier between you and any sexual partners. Do not share needles or any other items for using drugs.

- There are no vaccines for HIV as of yet because of its high amount of variability. However, PrEP and PEP can prevent people who may be exposed or who have been exposed to HIV contamination from developing the disease.

- If you choose to practise risky behaviors, get tested at least once a year for HIV. Do not wait until the symptoms of AIDS appear before checking to see if you have the disease.

Chapter Three

How is HIV/AIDS Diagnosed?

What tests do they have for HIV/AIDS?

Blood tests are the standard test for HIV. There are also saliva tests and urine tests. Of the three, urine tests are the least accurate. The first test usually performed to see whether someone is HIV-positive is an ELISA (enzyme-linked immunosorbant assay), which is also called an EIA (enzyme immunoassay). For this test, HIV is anchored to a solid. The blood to be tested is washed over the HIV solid. If you have HIV and your body has begun to produce antibodies (between four weeks and six months after exposure), the antibodies in your blood will attach to the HIV. When the rest of your blood is rinsed off, the antibodies will remain attached to the HIV imbedded in the solid. Then a secondary antibody that will attach to HIV antibodies is washed over the solid. Again the solid is rinsed, so that only those antibodies that are attached remain. Finally, a chemical is added to make the secondary antibodies change colour. If any of the secondary antibodies have attached to the solid through the HIV antibodies, it will show up by changing colours.

'Blood tests are the standard test for HIV.'

Some ELISA tests, called rapid tests, take as little as 20 minutes to receive results; others require a few days. A negative test does not necessarily mean you do not have HIV. You may be in the initial range where you are not producing enough antibodies to register on the test and should be retested within six months.

After the initial diagnosis, HIV tests are usually sent to another lab to be tested with a Western Blot. A Western Blot also relies on the fact that HIV antibodies produced by your body want to grab onto HIV antigens. With a Western Blot test, the sample is watched as it moves through a thick gel. Electricity is used to power its movement, but it gets stuck if it grabs onto one of the antigens. It is possible for the Western Blot to come back with inconclusive results. Inconclusive results are neither positive nor negative; they just mean that the test needs to be repeated. Think of inconclusive results as if they are a football game that finished with a tie.

If you believe you have been recently exposed to HIV, you should be tested. If your test comes back negative, it is a good idea to repeat the test in a few months. There are tests that can be performed in the earliest stages of infection, which measure the actual HIV in your blood. RNA tests look for the genetic material of HIV in your blood.

These tests are not always useful since they become inaccurate within the first four weeks after infection. If there are any antibodies for HIV in your bloodstream, even at levels so small they are not detected by other tests, the antibodies will ruin the outcome of this test. The only time this test is used to diagnose HIV is if you know you have had recent risky contact with a known HIV-positive person, it is beyond the time for you to be able to use a PEP, and the ELISA and Western Blot both came back negative.

'If you believe you have been recently exposed to HIV, you should be tested. If your test comes back negative, it is a good idea to repeat the test in a few months.'

Home testing

Some home HIV testing kits are sold over the Internet. The accuracy of many of these kits is unknown. It is not recommended you use at-home test kits to determine your HIV status. If you are HIV-positive, you will need to find a healthcare professional to work with for treatment. It is a good idea to have the healthcare professional you trust perform your test.

How accurate is my diagnosis?

The accuracy of a HIV test depends on when you were potentially exposed to HIV. If you have been exposed recently and are feeling sick, it is okay to be tested for preliminary results. There is little data on the accuracy of antibody tests within the first four weeks after exposure. This is because everybody responds differently to the virus. Some people begin making antibodies in a few weeks; others take longer. It is called seroconversion when a person begins to make antibodies for a virus. A test performed three months after exposure is 97% accurate. A test performed six months after exposure is about 100% accurate.

False positive results

There are reasons you could get a false positive on an ELISA test. Because the ELISA test uses an antigen that Lyme disease, syphilis and lupus antibodies can also grab, people with these diseases may have an ELISA test that looks positive. Because the Western Blot measures more than just the ability of the antibody to grab the HIV antigen, it is more accurate.

P24 antigen tests, or RNA tests, look directly at the amount of HIV in your bloodstream. These tests are useful in the weeks before HIV antibodies can be detected, but then lose their usefulness as the HIV goes into hiding.

My doctor said I had AIDS before he did a blood test. Why?

Certain infections that occur only in people with a severely damaged immune system can signal to a doctor that a patient has AIDS. Frequently, these are called co-infections or opportunistic infections. A co-infection is when a person has more than one disease at a time. An opportunistic infection is when the second disease can only make people sick if they have the first infection.

Normally, your immune system would fight these AIDS-defining infections without making you ill. When your body is no longer able to fight them because of the damage to your immune system, these diseases attack and can be a person's first symptom of a HIV infection. Unfortunately, by the time these symptoms appear the disease has already progressed to AIDS.

Any diagnosis of HIV or AIDS should be confirmed with a blood test. If the test is positive and the disease has already progressed to AIDS, the physician should order more blood tests to better monitor it and define plans of treatment.

'It is not recommended you use at-home test kits to determine your HIV status.'

What is a CD4 count?

A CD4 count measures how many CD4+ T-cells are concentrated in your blood. The CD4 test is the standard measure for determining how well your treatment is working and when it is time to switch treatments. It is a good estimate of how well your immune system is functioning at any given time. CD4 can also be used to discover when HIV has caused AIDS. Normally, your body has between 500-1,800 cells/mm³. It is a good idea to begin treatment before your level drops to 350 cells/mm³. You will have a better chance of successful treatment.

Numbers alone do not determine where you are in your therapy. CD4 measurements are checked for trends and percentages, not strictly for numbers. They can help a physician determine when to start HIV therapy or if you are in need of preventative medicine to protect you from opportunistic infections.

'A test performed three months after exposure is 97% accurate. A test performed six months after exposure is about 100% accurate.'

What is a viral load?

The viral load is the amount of virus present in your blood. Usually viral load is measured periodically while you are on a treatment plan to ensure it is working effectively. An RNA test for HIV is used to measure your viral load. There must be more than 40 copies of the virus per mm³ of blood in order for it to be counted. If you have a level less than this, it means your treatment is doing its job. It is frequently called an undetectable amount of virus in your blood. It does not mean that you no longer have HIV. For reference, some people have had millions of copies of the virus per mm³.

What other kinds of tests will I need if I am HIV-positive?

If you are diagnosed with HIV, you should seek the care of a HIV clinic specialist or a genitourinary medicine (GUM) clinic. There, your healthcare provider will need to establish a baseline blood level for you. He or she will take several blood tests to see what the levels of your body chemistry are before you get sicker. These levels will allow your blood to be monitored for changes.

A change can inform your physician of a need for a different treatment, if you are developing an opportunistic infection or if you need more nutrients to replace those lost from therapy. Blood tests done throughout the course of your treatment will determine how well your body is responding to the medicine and how well the virus is responding.

Aside from a CD4 test and a viral load test, you may also need a HIV-resistant test. This is a test that will examine the HIV you have and determine if it is resistant to any of the drugs your doctor wants you to take. It is generally used at the beginning of your treatment, but it may also be used when you change treatments to ensure they are effective.

Other common blood tests that monitor body functions are: the full blood count (FBC), the liver function test, and the kidney function test. The FBC will check to see if your body is responding to an infection and may allow your doctor to treat you for co-infections before they get out of hand for your immune system to control. A full blood count will also tell your doctor if the medicines you are taking are becoming toxic to you. A liver function test is important when you are on certain medications or if you have hepatitis. The liver function test warns doctors if you need to change your medications because they are damaging your liver. They also will tell your doctor if you develop hepatitis. Some medications are dangerous for your kidneys, but high blood pressure and diabetes can also cause problems with your kidneys. A kidney function test will inform your doctor if your kidneys are being damaged or if you need to change medications.

'Any diagnosis of HIV or AIDS should be confirmed with a blood test.'

You may require tests that are not blood tests as symptoms develop. For example, your doctor may want you to have a bone density tests if you have been breaking bones easily or CT scans if you are having problems with your liver. You also should continue with standard tests, such as Pap smears, as your doctor recommends. Early diagnostic tests are important for keeping ahead of co-infections.

What are the four stages of HIV?

The World Health Organization has assigned four stages to HIV. The symptoms are characteristic of what a person in that stage may expect to experience. These lists are not exhaustive, and a person does not have to have all of them to be in that stage.

Clinical Stage I:

- There are no real symptoms at this stage.
- Enlarged lymph nodes.

Clinical Stage II:

- Moderate weight loss with no other known cause.
- Mouth ulcers.
- Herpes outbreaks. Most people have a dormant form of herpes in their bodies. When your immune system is weakened, it allows the herpes to become active. Herpes outbreaks that are caused by a HIV infection will last longer and occur more frequently than herpes infections in healthy people.
- Repeated infections of the nose, throat and lungs (tonsillitis, ear infections, sinus infections). Although your immune system has not collapsed during Stage II, it will have a more difficult time fighting simpler infections.
- Fungus infections in your fingernails and toenails.
- Skin cracks in the corner of your mouth.
- Flaky skin and rashes on the upper body and face that are itchy and inflamed are a symptom of seborrheic dermatitis, which is caused by overproduction of oil and a yeast infection.
- Bumpy skin eruptions that itch caused by infected hair follicles.

'The World Health Organization has assigned four stages to HIV.'

Clinical Stage III:

- Severe weight loss (more than 10% of original body weight) that has no other known cause.

- Persistent thrush (oral yeast infections caused by candidiasis).

- Pre-cancerous hairy white patches inside the mouth.

- Diarrhoea that lasts longer than a month and has no other known cause.

- Severe infections from bacteria.

- Anaemia (low red blood cells) with no other known cause.

- Fever that lasts for a month or longer with no other known cause.

- Mouth inflammation that leads to cells dying.

- Tuberculosis (TB) in the lungs. Tuberculosis is caused by bacteria and infects the lungs. Its unique symptoms are coughing up blood and night sweats. Coughing, fever, fatigue, shortness of breath, weight loss and occasionally chest pains are also symptoms. People who have been exposed to TB years earlier or people who recovered from TB can develop it when their immune system is down.

Clinical Stage IV

- AIDS pneumonias. Symptoms of pneumonia are fever, fatigue, shortness of breath and a dry cough. Pneumonias that are unique to AIDS patients usually occur when the patient's CD4 count is below 200 cells/mm^3.

- AIDS cancers (Kaposi's sarcoma, invasive cervical cancer, brain, non-Hodgkin's lymphoma). Certain cancers only appear in people who have damaged immune systems. Kaposi's sarcoma is a cancer that is one of the confirming diseases for AIDS. Symptoms of Kaposi's sarcoma are spots on the skin that are usually reddish or purple, but could also be brown or black.

- Wasting syndrome, which is characterised by a loss of both fat and muscle, is common in AIDS patients who have reached Stage IV.

- Tuberculosis outside of the lungs. When the immune system is completely weakened, TB no longer remains inside the lungs. It travels to and infects other organs.

- MAC (mycobacterium avium complex). MAC is related to TB but is not contagious to most people. The symptoms of a MAC infection are a fever that is cyclic or continuous, loss of appetite and weight loss, night sweats, swollen glands, weakness or fatigue, diarrhoea, and abdominal pain. An AIDS patient's CD4 count is usually below 50 cells/mm^3 when they are susceptible to this disease.

- Brain diseases caused by co-infections that enter the brain and cause altered states of mind (such as toxoplasmosis leading to encephalopathy and leukoencephalopathy).

- Chronic herpes outbreaks that last longer than a month.

- Thrush that migrates into the esophagus (yeast infection in the throat – candidiasis). A person with AIDS who has an oral yeast infection and begins having difficulty swallowing and throat pain should contact their doctor immediately.

- Blood poisoning (septicaemia).

- AIDS-related protozoan infection (leishmaniasis). Transmitted by the sandfly, it generally causes ulcers on the skin but can infect all body systems.

- AIDS-related kidney and heart disease.

- Invasive cervical cancer.

- Skin infections on the skin of organs and the eyes (cytomegalovirus). Symptoms of an eye infection are blind spots or loss of peripheral vision, seeing floating spots or flashes, and headaches. This only attacks those with a CD4 count of less than 50 cells/mm^3.

- Fungal brain infection (cryptococcosis). Symptoms include headache, fever, chest pain, dry cough, nausea and vomiting, fatigue, blurred vision and confusion. A CD4 count of less than 100 cells/mm3 is usually necessary for cryptococcis to cause problems.

- Severe diarrhoea caused by protozoan infections of the intestines (cryptosporidiosis).

Summing Up

- There are several tests that can be done to detect if a person is infected with HIV. ELISA tests with a Western Blot follow-up are the most common and are most accurate after six months.

- If the diagnostic tests are performed six months after the time of infection, they are 100% accurate. If they are performed sooner, they are less accurate.

- The presence of co-infections that only seem to make people with AIDS sick can alert a doctor that you may have AIDS. Tests should be performed immediately to confirm the disease if you have a co-infection typical of AIDS.

- A CD4 test can help your doctor monitor the progress of your disease. The CD4 test should be watched for trends not numbers.

- A viral load is the amount of virus present in your blood. Viral loads are another way to test how a HIV-positive person is responding to treatment.

- There are several tests that a HIV-positive person needs to have at regular intervals. In addition to monitoring their immune system and viral load, the other body systems will have to be tested to watch for negative side effects from treatment.

- The World Health Organization (WHO) has designated four stages of AIDS that are characterised by certain symptoms. These symptoms make it easier for doctors to catagorise patients without initial tests.

Chapter Four

Current HIV/AIDS Treatments

How do HIV/AIDS medicines work?

A person taking HIV medicines to fight AIDS is said to be taking or doing antiretroviral therapy (ART). Antiretroviral therapy is the combination of medicines used to fight against AIDS. The goal of antiretroviral therapy is to provide enough medicine to prevent HIV from reproducing without preventing your cells from carrying on the tasks necessary to keep them alive. Medicines are more effective than your own body at defending against HIV because they can get inside the cells where the virus hides.

Medicines interfere with the ability of HIV to make copies in several ways. The medicines can prevent the tool that copies HIV from RNA to DNA from working, they can interfere with the making of the tools HIV needs to carry with it, they can prevent HIV's DNA from attaching to your cell's DNA, and they can prevent HIV from entering the cell. Different medicines act in different ways and combining them helps improve their effectiveness.

Most doctors use antiretroviral therapy as a part of maintenance therapy. Maintenance therapy is designed to keep an AIDS patient in a stable state of health. Aside from drugs that keep HIV in check, maintenance therapy may include drugs to keep co-infections and opportunistic infections under control as well.

'A person taking HIV medicines to fight AIDS is said to be taking or doing antiretroviral therapy (ART).'

What are some of the antiretroviral drugs?

Antiretroviral drugs are medicines that are used to fight against retroviruses like HIV. There are five major classes of antiretroviral drugs at this time and each of them functions in a unique way to prevent HIV from making more copies of itself.

At one point in time, antiretroviral drugs were used one at a time until they no longer worked. This was thought to extend the life of the patient. Now, combination therapy, or the use of two or more drugs at the same time is recognised as the most effective way of fighting HIV. With the development of this new therapy, some drug companies have combined more than one antiretroviral drug into one pill to make the number of pills patients have to take lower.

Since each antiretroviral drug can have up to four names (the chemical name, the generic name, the brand name and the abbreviation) only the generic names and abbreviations are listed. Because combination drugs are usually too new to have a generic name, their brand name and the abbreviations of the other drugs in it are given.

'The goal of antiretroviral therapy is to provide enough medicine to prevent HIV from reproducing without preventing your cells from carrying on the tasks necessary to keep them alive.'

Most common ART drugs

Here are some of the major drugs from each class of antiretroviral drugs:

- Combination therapy drugs: Atripla (EFV & TDF & FTC), Kivexa (ABC & 3TC), Truvada (TDF & FTC), and Combivir (AZT & 3TC).

- Nucleoside reverse transcriptase inhibitors: emtricitabine (FTC), lamivudine (3TC), zidovudine (AZT or ZDV), didanosine (ddI), tenofovir (TDF), and abacavir (ABC).

- Non-nucleoside reverse transcriptase inhibitors: efavirenz (EFV) and nevirapine (NVP).

- Protease inhibitors: tipranavir (TPV), indinavir (IDV), saquinavir (SQV), fosamprenavir (FOS-APV), amprenavir (APV), ritonavir (RTV), darunavir (DRV), and nelfinavir (NFV).

- Entry or fusion inhibitors: enfuvirtide (T-20), and maraviroc (MVC).

- Integrase inhibitors: raltegravir (RAL).

All of these drugs are used as a starting regimen in the UK except for the entry or fusion inhibitors and the integrase inhibitors. These categories of drugs are used only after an initial course of treatment needs to be changed. This list does not contain all the possible drugs, and new ones are constantly being developed.

Nucleoside reverse transcriptase inhibitor (NRTI)

A nucleoside is a building block for making genetic material. Reverse transciptase is the name of a protein tool that turns RNA into DNA. Inhibitor means it prevents it from working. A nucleoside reverse transcriptase inhibitor (NRTI) sometimes called a nucleoside analog, is a medicine that looks like a nucleoside and prevents the tool HIV uses for turning RNA into DNA from finishing the DNA.

A virus like HIV is called a retrovirus because it is made from RNA and must be turned into DNA in order to work and make more copies of itself. Retroviruses are unique because in every other natural system DNA makes RNA and more DNA. RNA in regular systems cannot make DNA; it makes proteins. Since retroviruses go against the normal process, an RNA virus must come with a special tool in order to do this. This tool is called reverse transcriptase. This tool can build DNA from RNA.

In order to work, reverse transcriptase sits on the RNA and travels down it like a train on a track. With each of the genes it sees on the RNA, it grabs the DNA building block equivalent and attaches it to the end of the chain of DNA it is making. The reverse transcriptase for HIV works by putting together a DNA puzzle.

The RNA is the picture of the puzzle and the DNA is the puzzle. An NRTI is like a puzzle piece that is the wrong shape. When you are putting a puzzle together, you can force the wrong piece into a spot where you have become frustrated. However, if you do this, the puzzle will not look right and have gaps. When you are taking the NRTI, it works because it is easier to find an NRTI than it is to find the right puzzle piece – a nucleoside.

When the DNA is made with the wrong piece, the NRTI acts like an ending corner on the puzzle and no more pieces can be attached to it. Because HIV must turn into a complete DNA copy in order to make more of itself, an NRTI prevents HIV from reproducing.

Non-nucleoside reverse transcriptase inhibitor (NNRTI)

An NNRTI also prevents the tool that turns HIV RNA into DNA from working. The difference is how the drug works. While an NRTI works by becoming a part of the new DNA chain and making it so nothing else can be added to it, an NNRTI attaches to the tool and prevents it from working. With a non-nucleoside reverse transcriptase inhibitor, the puzzle piece attaches to the reverse transcriptase tool. It is as if the train wheels are locked and the train can no longer sit on the track. With a puzzle piece blocking the place for RNA, the tool cannot attach to the RNA and begin making a copy of it.

Protease inhibitor (PI)

Protease is a tool the cell uses to make other proteins. In order for a protein to work, it must be cut and shaped. The job of protease is to cut proteins. If proteins are not cut into the right shape they will not work, just like a key that is shaped wrong will not work.

Like other inhibitor drugs, a protease inhibitor prevents protease from working. When the protease that cuts proteins for HIV is blocked it cannot do its job. The proteins that are prevented from being cut do not work correctly. By not allowing the proteins to work for the HIV, you prevent them from helping HIV reproduce.

Integrase inhibitor

Integrase is another tool that works like a tailor for HIV. It cuts your DNA and sews HIV's DNA into the hole. When HIV turns into its DNA form, it can only make more HIV if it tricks your cell into working for it. It does this by slipping

'Because HIV must turn into a complete DNA copy in order to make more of itself, an NRTI prevents HIV from reproducing.'

into your DNA, so that your cell thinks it is its own DNA. If you take a medicine that prevents integrase from working properly, HIV's DNA cannot get into the DNA of your cell and make more of itself.

Entry or fusion inhibitor

All of the drugs on the market for fighting HIV prevent the virus from making more of itself. Most of them block the process of reproduction inside the cell, but fusion inhibitors work to prevent HIV from even entering the cell. Every cell in your body has binding proteins on its cell membrane. Binding proteins are little key-like fingers that lock onto the things a cell needs. Sadly, HIV looks like something CD4 needs to grab. When HIV is present, the CD4 finger will lock onto the HIV and bring it into the cell.

Entry or fusion inhibitors will attach to CD4 so that HIV cannot attach there. They may also lock onto a spot next to CD4 and make it so that HIV cannot reach the CD4 binding site through fusion inhibitor. Some entry or fusion inhibitors can also attach to the HIV on the spot that CD4 will grab. This makes it so the CD4 cannot attach to the HIV. All entry or fusion inhibitors prevent HIV from entering your T-cells.

What is combination therapy?

Combination therapy is a form of HIV therapy that uses at least three different HIV drugs. Highly active antiretroviral therapy (HAART) is combination therapy that also uses two different classes of the drugs. Because the drugs are not only hitting HIV from different angles but at different stages in its development, combination therapy has proven to be highly effective in keeping HIV reproduction under control for longer periods of time.

Although combination therapy is effective, some doctors use a class-sparing approach to treating AIDS. If a doctor uses a class-sparing treatment, he or she will not use one class of HIV drug until all other treatments have failed. For example, a doctor may not use integrase inhibitor drugs as a part of your treatment until all other treatments stop working.

'Combination therapy is a form of HIV therapy that uses at least three different HIV drugs.'

Why do I have to keep changing my medicine all the time?

HIV is careless when it makes copies, but eventually it changes so that the medicines you are using are no longer effective. In addition, while all the careless forms of HIV die, the stronger forms that can avoid the affects of the drugs you are taking will survive. This means the next generation of HIV will be the same as the stronger type that was able to make more of itself. Although viruses are completely dependent on cells for reproduction, there have been documented cases of viruses sharing information. If one virus can avoid a specific drug, and it shares this information with another virus, that virus will also be able to avoid the drug.

To better fight HIV, your doctor may order a genotypic assay or a phenotypic assay.

A phenotypic assay looks at how the virus responds to certain drugs in the lab. It takes two to three weeks, and its results are easier to understand. When the doctor is having trouble treating HIV or if the form of HIV being treated has multiple resistances, than the phenotypic assay is the best test to perform.

The genotypic assay just looks at the genes of the HIV. This assay is quicker, but its results are a little more difficult to understand. It provides the same information as a phenotypic assay.

'If you choose to use alternative medicines, it is imperative that you find a person who is trained and certified in providing the therapy you choose.'

Is there a natural way to fight HIV/AIDS?

Modern medicines are highly effective against HIV. Because of this, there is usually no reason to choose alternative forms of dealing with the disease over current medically approved methods unless ART or HAART stops working. Alternative medicines can be effective in treating side effects and dealing with the stress of receiving a HIV diagnosis, but all care needs to be coordinated between healthcare professionals.

Because there are few standardised methods of performing alternative therapies, it makes them difficult to test scientifically. Their effectiveness is often troublesome to predict. If you choose to use alternative medicines, it is imperative that you find a person who is trained and certified in providing the therapy you choose. The practitioner should be sympathetic to your disease and listen when you talk to him or her. He or she should accept the use of alternative and modern medicine together. It is helpful if he or she has experience with AIDS patients.

Alternative medicine

Here are some of the types of alternative medicine and what the research has shown so far about their effectiveness:

- Acupuncture – A trained acupuncturist inserts needles into different points on your skin. Acupuncture seems effective against some pain and nerve-related issues.

- Herbs – Plant substances are used like medicines. Some modern medicines came into existence because they were originally extracted from plants. Be alert for drug interactions if you are taking herbs. Try to find a reputable (preferably certified) person who makes and distributes them.

- Homeopathy – Uses diluted herbs and partial natural treatments to correct problems. Homeopathy has not shown to be effective beyond the therapeutic effect of talking to someone about your problems.

- Naturopathy – A combination of diet, acupuncture, herbs and massage. These therapies have shown positive results when used individually. As with anything that uses herbs, inform all your healthcare providers about what you are using and when you use it.

- Chinese medicine – A combination of herbs, acupuncture and massage. Similar results to those of naturopathy. Inform your healthcare providers about herb supplements and watch for drug interactions.

- Ayurveda or Indian medicine – This uses a variety of different techniques including, yoga, massage, cleansing procedures, herbs, diet and meditation. Some of the individual techniques have positive results, some have not been tested, and some may cause negative results. Again, be sure to inform your healthcare providers of the treatments you are using.

- Meditation, relaxation, visualisation and prayer – Work on the basis that the mind is a powerful healer. The fact that placebos with no medicinal benefit can help some people is evidence that this works, but keep in mind the placebo effect is usually minimal. These techniques have been shown to help with pain and stress.

- Yoga, tai chi and qigong – These combine light exercise with meditation techniques and have similar results to meditation. They are different from meditation because they are usually performed in a group, so you get the added support of the group.

- Vitamins, minerals, pro-biotics, pre-biotics, animal extracts, and supplements – These are used to help give your body the nutrition that your regular diet may be lacking. Used to supplement your diet, vitamin A, riboflavin (B2), pyridoxine (B6), cobalamin (B12), biotin, folic acid (folate), niacin, pantothenic acid, vitamin E, cadmium, chromium, iron, selenium, zinc and protein, have shown to be effective in maintaining a healthy immune system for AIDS patients. If you use them in high doses, they can interfere with your treatment and some may cause harm.

- Massage therapy, Shiatsu (Japanese massage) and acupressure – Uses the manipulation of muscles to reduce pain. If your pain is muscle based, these can be helpful. In general, they help to relieve mental stress.

- Reiki – This is a method of manipulating the energy of the body. There have been few studies done on its effectiveness.

- Bioelectromagnetic therapy – Uses magnets, sound, light and other energy forms and sources to encourage healing. Some things, such as light therapy for those who are depressed, have shown positive results, but this is another area that has not been tested extensively.

New research

The research for ways to prevent HIV, reduce the effects of co-infections, fight HIV, and find a cure, cover a wide range of methods of attack:

- Minocycline is a drug that has been used to control acne. It was found to reduce the activity of T-cells. Because it reduces the general production of T-cells, it is thought that integrating this antibiotic as part of combination therapy would make it even more effective. The idea to use this drug came from a test on monkeys with SIV (a monkey or simian form of HIV). Scientists think it will work because when T-cells are inactive and resting they do not produce HIV.

* Immune therapy is another area of current research. With immune therapy, the drugs are used to help boost the immune system. Several drugs are being researched, and all of them are in different stages of development.

* In the area of gene therapy, scientists hope to remove T-cells from HIV patients, adjusting the DNA to prevent HIV from using it, and then putting the T-cells back inside the patient.

* A universal vaccine to prevent the disease is still a long way off, but therapeutic vaccines could work as an alternative to combination therapy and HAART. A therapeutic vaccine injects HIV antibodies into the patient to help reduce the amount of HIV. Some also inject HIV material or even bacteria into the person to create a strong immune response.

* Microbicides are the next line of defense against the spread of AIDS. Microbicides are creams or gels that will destroy any virus they contact.

* One AIDS patient had surgery to remove his infected T-cells. Twice, adult stem cells were transplanted into him from a non-infected donor with a mutation that might make the cells resistant to HIV infection. The AIDS patient was also treated with radiation and chemotherapy. This AIDS patient has not taken antiretroviral drugs since 2007, but seems to have contained the disease. Less rigorous treatments with patients remaining on ART have also shown positive results.

'Immune therapy is another area of current research. With immune therapy, the drugs are used to help boost the immune system.'

Summing Up

- HIV treatments work by interfering with the virus' ability to reproduce. They exploit the careless work that the virus does. They also prevent the virus from entering the cell.

- There are five different classes of antiretroviral medicines approved at this time. They are: NRTIs, NNRTIs, protease inhibitors, HAART combination drugs, and fusion inhibitors.

- NRTIs are nucleoside reverse transcriptase inhibitors. They work by knocking reverse transcriptase off RNA so it cannot be turned into DNA.

- NNRTIs or non-nucleoside reverse transcriptase inhibitors work by attaching themselves to the reverse transcriptase and preventing it from attaching to the RNA of HIV.

- PIs are protease inhibitors. These medicines prevent proteins in the cell from working for HIV.

- Fusion inhibitors work by preventing HIV from binding to T-cells. They can either bind to the same site as HIV or get in the way of the site so HIV cannot reach it.

- Integrase inhibitors were created to prevent HIV from become a part of the T-cell DNA. When the HIV's DNA cannot enter the cell's DNA, it is not reproduced.

- Combination therapy and HAART are ways of dealing with HIV using multiple drugs across classes. They have proven highly effective in keeping HIV at bay for many years at a time.

- In order to keep on top of the ever-changing HIV, drug therapies and medicines must change as the virus becomes resistant to treatments.

- Alternative therapies can be beneficial for helping control side effects, but should not replace modern medical treatments unless there is no other course of treatment. Always choose a person who has been trained and certified in the form of alternative medicine they practise.

- New methods and medicines to deal with HIV are on the horizon. Treatments of the future range from drugs to boost or replace current therapies to drugs to help prevent the spread of HIV from one person to the next.

Chapter Five

Side Effects of HIV/ AIDS Treatments

What are the common side effects of HIV/AIDS medicines?

There are some side effects that many people being treated for HIV develop. Most of these side effects are troublesome, but can be handled. Discuss all side effects with your physician. If you experience side effects that you feel you cannot handle, consult your doctor to see if there are alternative treatment plans that will reduce or remove the side effects that are bothering you. Here are some common side effects and advice on how to deal with them:

Weight loss:

- It is essential for any HIV-positive person to purchase accurate scales, regardless of cost. They need to plot their weight on a chart every day. Each morning as soon as you wake up, go to the bathroom, take off your clothes and weigh yourself. Do not drink anything before you weigh yourself, and protect your scale so it does not get damaged. Tell your doctor if, on average, you notice you are losing or gaining weight.

- Never go on a diet to lose weight when you have AIDS. No one is happy with the way his or her body looks. AIDS can amplify your bad spots. Do not try to change them. Ideally, AIDS patients should maintain their weight without losing or gaining.

'If you experience side effects that you feel you cannot handle, consult your doctor to see if there are alternative treatment plans that will reduce or remove the side effects that are bothering you.'

- Drink nutritional supplements between meals or make your own from a protein source (like soy protein), a dairy source and fruit.

- Eat high-protein and high-calorie foods such as peanut butter, pasteurised cottage cheese, tuna, salmon, hard pasteurised cheeses, yoghurt and eggs. Add protein powders to your foods, such as soups and sauces, when you cook.

- Prepare foods and dishes that are colourful and smell appetising.

- AIDS patients should try to eat 14 to 16 calories per pound of normal weight. A person whose normal weight is 180 pounds should eat between 2,520-2,880 calories per day.

Fatigue:

- Get some exercise. Force yourself to take a walk each day.

- Keep regular sleeping hours that will make it so your body does not have to change its sleep times with daylight saving time. Ask your doctor how many hours of sleep are recommended and set your sleep time based on their recommendation.

- Purchase foods that require no preparation to make so you can still eat when you are tired.

- Have your doctor check to see if you are anaemic.

- Keep a balanced diet.

Dry mouth:

- Drink plenty of liquids throughout the day.

- Drink liquorice tea or slippery elm tea.

- Suck on ice chips or sugar-free hard sweets.

- Ask your doctor about a glycerine lemon mouth rinse or artificial saliva.

- Eat foods that contain high amounts of liquid, and avoid dry foods such as breads and bananas.

Diarrhoea:

- Practise good sanitation. Wash your hands frequently. Keep raw meat and utensils separate from cooked meat and utensils. Always cook foods thoroughly.
- Do not overuse antacids.
- Eat more soluble fibre. If you take a fibre supplement such as psyllium without water, you can help your diarrhoea, but you will need to talk with your physician before you do this. Taking too much soluble fibre without taking in enough liquid can cause serious bowel conditions.
- Drink buttermilk or eat yoghurt.
- Stay hydrated while you are experiencing diarrhoea by drinking oral rehydration solutions. Water on its own can cause problems and so can salt pills. Trying to make your own rehydration solution at home is not recommended.
- Eat more bananas.

Nausea and vomiting:

- Ginger tea, gingerbread, and other products that contain real ginger can help reduce nausea.
- Peppermint tea and peppermint sweets can help reduce nausea.
- Sipping very cold, clear, carbonated beverages such as ginger ale can help.
- Do not cook foods with strong smells such as cabbage.
- Use oral rehydration solutions to keep yourself hydrated if you are vomiting frequently.
- Eat small frequent meals with soft, bland foods such as apple sauce, mashed rice, or mashed potatoes. Stay away from greasy foods or foods high in fat.
- Ask your doctor if you can take anti-nausea medications.

Headaches:

- Drink a glass of water.

- Find a good psychologist to talk to about the stress in your life.

- Lie down in a dark, quiet room.

- Get a massage on the back of your neck and lower skull by someone trained in acupressure.

- Ask a doctor what kind of over-the-counter medicine, such as paracetamol, ibuprofen or aspirin, would be best for you to take if you develop a headache.

Anaemia (low red blood cell count):

- Change your diet to include foods rich in iron, zinc, cobalamine (B12), and folic acid (folate).

- Ask your doctor about changing medicines.

- Take vitamin supplements.

'Always check for rashes after you start any new medication.'

Rashes (that have been confirmed by a doctor to not be life-threatening)**:**

- Always check for rashes after you start any new medication. Some rashes can be a symptom of an allergic reaction or serious condition. Tell your doctor whenever a rash appears. See your doctor immediately if your rash is inside your mouth, is accompanied by difficulty breathing, is on the palms of your hands or soles of your feet, or has blisters. Ask your doctor if you can keep an adrenaline injection or other medication on hand to take if you have an allergic reaction. If he or she agrees, learn how and when to use this medication from them.

- Stay out of the sun.

- Choose cleansers for your skin that are glycerine based *and* hypoallergenic.

- Do not apply products to your skin that contain fragrances.

- Bathe in lukewarm water. Water that is too hot can dry the skin and make rashes worse.

50

Hair loss:

- Stress, as well as HIV medicines, can cause hair loss. Try to reduce stress through alternative therapies or psychotherapies.

- Ask your doctor about medications that will help your hair to grow back.

- To help prevent hair loss, do not have your hair chemically permed, dyed, or straightened while you are taking HIV medications.

- Be careful when combing or brushing your hair, start at the ends and move upward little by little until you get to your scalp.

- Do not wear hairstyles that involve pulling your hair tight, such as braids.

Long-term side effects of HIV/AIDS medicines

There are some side effects you may develop while being treated for HIV and AIDS that initiate changes in your body and last for the rest of your life. While these changes can usually be managed, you need to keep your doctor informed if they happen to you.

- Diabetes – This is a disease where your body is no longer able to process sugars. Your chances of getting diabetes increase if you are overweight or if you have other complications such as liver problems. If you are on protease inhibitors, you should make sure your glucose levels are being monitored at your regular check-ups. Symptoms of diabetes are frequent urination, unexplained rapid weight loss, excessive thirst, blurred vision, numbness in your extremities, irritability and sores that are slow to heal. Diabetes can be regulated through diet and/or medication. Type I diabetes can be caused because your medications or HIV harms your pancreas so insulin is no longer produced. Type I diabetes cannot be reversed. Type II diabetes is caused because your body develops a resistance to the insulin it produces. Type II diabetes can be reversed through weight loss, healthy diet and exercise.

- Osteopenia, osteoporosis, osteonecrosis – These are all diseases of the bone. Osteopenia is a loss of bone density, which leads to osteoporosis. Osteoporosis is a condition where you have lost so much of your bone mass that your bones are beginning to break. Osteonecrosis is when the blood supply to a bone is so low that it kills a portion of the bone. Most conditions dealing with bone will not occur if you get enough calcium and vitamin D in your diet. Maintaining a steady weight and getting enough exercise are also good ways to prevent bone loss. Reduce your alcohol and caffeine consumption and stop smoking. There are not warning signs of osteopenia and osteoporosis until a broken bone occurs. A bone mass density (BMD) can be performed to test your bone density if you or your doctor are concerned about these conditions. Usually the head of the femur bone in the hip is the only bone to be affected by osteonecrosis. Tell your doctor if you have pain in your hip joint.

- Lipodystrophy – This is a disease where the fat in your body disappears from one place and reappears in another place. Generally, fat is lost from the cheeks, buttocks, arms and legs. Fat is gained around your stomach and on the back of your neck. It is a common side effect and can lead to higher levels of cholesterol in the blood, and diabetes. Some people confuse wasting disease and lipodystrophy. People with wasting disease lose weight from all over their bodies and lose muscle as well as fat. People with lipodystrophy simply move the fat around from one place to another without losing weight. To prevent lipodystrophy, change your diet, eat more fibre, and get exercise.

- Hyperlipidaemia – This is a condition where your blood cholesterol increases. It occurs when people with HIV are using protease inhibitors. Your doctor will take blood tests to monitor your blood cholesterol levels. To correct the condition you will need to change your diet, quit smoking, and exercise. There are also medicines your physician may prescribe to correct the issue.

- Peripheral neuropathy – 30% of people who are HIV-positive get this condition where the nerves in the extremities begin to break down. It is uncertain whether HIV infecting nerve cells or the medicine causes this. If it is caused by the medicine and you change medicine, it may take up to eight weeks for the condition to improve. Symptoms are stiffness and numbness, pins and needles, burning sensation in the extremities, trouble walking or standing, tickling, pain, and sensations that are more intense that usual. One way to deal with the pain is by asking your doctor for medication. Also, B vitamins are beneficial for repairing nerves. Other ways that might be helpful are: soaking extremities in ice water, choosing slippers and shoes that are loose, not standing or walking for long periods of time and keeping your extremities uncovered at night. Massage therapy or acupuncture may also help.

Dangerous side effects of HIV/AIDS medicines

There are some dangerous side effects people may develop while being treated for HIV and AIDS. Following your treatment plan and keeping an open line of communication between you and your doctor is very important. It will help you and your doctor recognise serious side effects and control them before they become dangerous. If you have symptoms of any of the following conditions, seek immediate medical treatment.

A life-threatening rash (caused by an allergy to the medicine):

- A rash with breathing difficulties.
- A rash that has red spots with blisters in the centre of them, or any rash that blisters.
- A rash inside your mouth, on the soles of your feet or on the palms of your hands.
- A rash that causes your skin to peel.
- A rash with a fever or headache.
- A rash accompanied by a general feeling of sickness.

Hepatotoxicity (liver damage):

- Hepatotoxicity is usually detected in its early stages by monitoring your blood chemistry. If you are taking a drug that can increase your chances of developing liver damage, you will need to have your chemistry checked every two weeks for up to three months.
- It is the job of your liver to clean your bloodstream. Because the medicines

'Following your treatment plan and keeping an open line of communication between you and your doctor is very important. It will help you and your doctor recognise serious side effects and control them before they become dangerous.'

you take are not supposed to be in your blood naturally, the liver may work overtime to clean them from your bloodstream. When this happens, it can damage your liver.

- ▨ Symptoms of severe hepatotoxicity are the same as those associated with hepatitis: light stools, jaundice, nausea, vomiting, a general sick feeling, a tired or weak feeling, anorexia, and stomach pain.

- ▨ Because alcoholic beverages can speed up the stages of hepatotoxicity, it is recommended you drink no more than two drinks containing alcohol each day. This is true if you are on certain drugs or already have hepatotoxicity. People with severe damage to their liver should not consume alcoholic beverages. Talk to your doctor to find out if you need to limit your alcohol consumption.

Mitochondrial toxicity:

- ▨ Mitochondria are the energy generators located in every cell inside your body. NRTIs can damage your mitochondria and cause their numbers to decrease inside each cell.

- ▨ Symptoms of mitochondrial toxicity are: muscle weakness (myopathy) that gets worse, rapid breathing, sore muscles, nausea, vomiting, weight loss and fatigue.

- ▨ People with symptoms of mitochondrial toxicity should see their healthcare provider immediately.

I didn't feel sick until I started taking the medicine. Do I have to keep taking it?

HIV is a deadly virus. As with other deadly diseases, the only way to fight it is with medicines that are strong enough to hurt the disease. Unfortunately, these drugs sometimes have side effects on our bodies, too. The choice to stop taking your medicines is not like the choice to cut your hair. If you have long hair and you cut it short, it will eventually grow long again. However, if you stop taking your medicine, you will never get the added years back the medicine could have given you.

If you have severe side effects or ones that are very bothersome, you can speak to your doctor about them. It is possible that you can change your regimen or habits to improve the side effects.

Why do I have to keep getting blood tests?

Blood tests are an important way of monitoring HIV. When you are first diagnosed, it is important to get baseline information, so your doctor can weigh that against future results. It is crucial to keep track of blood signals that allow your doctors to monitor your internal organs while you are on medicine. In addition, it is vital that the levels of your CD4 and the viral loads are carefully observed in order to keep one step ahead of the disease.

Blood tests are not enjoyable, but neither is the daily news. They are the only information line into your body, and what they tell you and your doctors is very valuable.

What is immune reconstitution inflammatory syndrome (IRIS)?

Immune reconstitution inflammatory syndrome (IRIS), also known as immune reconstitution syndrome (IRS) or immune restoration disease (IRD), is a condition that appears in AIDS patients when their immune system rebounds. Because people who are HIV-positive have suppressed immune systems, their immune systems tend to ignore certain diseases. For example, if you have latent tuberculosis (TB) and your body is fighting HIV, it will ignore the TB. However, once you begin to take medicine that suppresses the HIV, your immune system will go into overdrive trying to attack the TB.

When your immune system goes into overdrive, your lymph nodes will swell. You will develop a fever, skin lesions, and potentially a rash. If you have a wound, it may swell and become red and tender. In extreme cases, your eyes will become inflamed, and you may notice changes in your rate of breathing. IRIS can be life-threatening, but it usually clears up in a few weeks.

'It is vital that the levels of your CD4 and the viral loads are carefully observed in order to keep one step ahead of the disease.'

You are more likely to develop IRIS if you start therapy for the first time with a severely damaged immune system (your CD4 is less than 100 cells/mm³). When you start therapy, if your viral load drops by about 100 times what it was, you have a good chance of getting IRIS. People with at least one opportunistic infection present also have a greater chance of developing IRIS even if the opportunistic infection has been controlled. It can also occur if you go off therapy and then decide to restart it.

If you are experiencing symptoms of IRIS, you can have your doctor do a blood test that measures your general immune system white blood cell count. If you need treatment because IRIS has become serious, your physician will either treat the opportunistic infection or treat the inflammation with non-steroidal anti-inflammatory drugs or corticosteriods. Another possible treatment is montelukast.

Drug-drug interactions

Unfortunately, medicine works by affecting how our body works. However, medicines can affect how other medicines work as well. It has been said that if you take more than ten different medicines, you can expect that some of them will interact with the others. As an AIDS patient, it is very possible you will need to take more than ten medicines. For this reason, you should always keep a list of what you are taking and when you take it with you. It is also helpful to keep a record of medicines you've taken in the past, how long you took them, and how they affected you. Make sure all your healthcare providers know what medicines you are taking at the beginning of each appointment and the last time you took each of them.

When drugs interact, they can do one of two things. First, they can work together so that the job they do is magnified. This is called synergy. Second, one drug can affect how much of another drug can get into the bloodstream. This can either make you have more than safe amounts of a drug in your blood, or it can make you have less than effective amounts in your blood.

When most people think about drug-drug interactions, they think about how one prescription drug interacts with another. While this is important, most doctors know how to work with drug-drug interactions of this kind. Dangerous drug-drug interactions can occur when a person takes non-prescription drugs

'Make sure all your healthcare providers know what medicines you are taking at the beginning of each appointment and the last time you took each of them.'

that their doctor doesn't know they have taken, herbs and alternative medicines, and can even be caused by everyday common things that most people do not see as drugs at all, such as caffeine and alcohol.

You should make an effort to keep track of the drugs you take and avoid possible interactions. Although it is primarily the job of your doctors to do this, an extra pair of eyes will only help the situation. These are some drugs that may interact with your HIV medicines:

- Stomach antacid drugs
- Some cholesterol drugs
- Migraine drugs
- Calcium channel blockers
- Anti-rejection drugs given after an organ transplant
- Oral contraceptives
- Drugs for erectile dysfunction
- Drugs given to fight opportunistic infections
- Amphetamines
- Opiates
- High doses of garlic
- St. John's wort

'Keeping a list of *all* the medicines you use is very important. It can help to prevent accidental drug-drug interactions.'

Keeping a list of *all* the medicines you use is very important. It can help to prevent accidental drug-drug interactions. It is also very important to use only healthcare providers who have experience with HIV drugs.

How long do I have to stay on my medicine?

Once you go on treatment therapy to control HIV, plan on being on it for decades. In the past, it was thought that stopping therapy for a drug holiday would boost the immune system. This was called a structured treatment interruption (STI). When patients began therapy with low CD4 counts or had trouble with therapy, they were taken off the medications for a few months. Some patients were also allowed to stop treatment if the side effects became difficult or even when patients became tired of the drug regimen.

Most of the research on this topic has shown negative results. People who begin a structured treatment interruption with a low CD4 count may raise them a little initially, but they quickly fall again.

People who take drug holidays have an increased chance of developing IRIS and dying, even if their CD4 levels remain high during the break. It was also found that taking breaks increased the resistant HIV so that some drugs stopped working on the virus. There have been a couple of studies, one in France and one in Switzerland, that showed positive results if the person who began a structured treatment interruption did so with a high CD4 count. For this reason, some people would like to have structured treatment interruptions studied, while others believe they are too dangerous to continue researching.

'The general consensus today is that the risk of stopping your medicine is greater than any benefit you might receive.'

The medicines people take to control HIV today are much improved over the drugs of yesterday. The general consensus today is that the risk of stopping your medicine is greater than any benefit you might receive. Do not stop taking your drugs unless your doctor agrees that you should stop. The only reasons a doctor should agree to this is if you are too sick to continue on medicine, you have agreed to participate in a structured treatment interruption study, or the side effects have become too serious.

Adherence

Adherence is the best policy with all HIV treatments. Adherence is when you willingly follow a treatment plan prescribed for you. People who are able to follow their regimen from the start do better than those who do not. Some of the problems with side effects can be eliminated or reduced if you are honest with your physician about any missed or troublesome doses, and you adhere to your treatment timetable.

People who have difficulty with adherence usually miss doses because:

■ They have overbooked their lives and are too busy.

■ They sleep through their dose time.

- They are having side effects from their medicines.
- They are depressed.
- They are on holiday away from home.
- They forget.

To do better job of adhering to your regimen you should:

- Always get a copy of your treatment plan. Place it with your pills in a place where it will be easy to remember.
- You can begin practising your regimen before you start treatment by using mints, small chocolates or jellybeans.
- If you find any part of your treatment plan to be difficult, talk it over with your doctor immediately.
- Always take your medications at the same time each day.
- Purchase a pillbox that allows you to keep each dose in a separate slot and allows you to set up your pills for an entire week.
- Create a medication diary. For a medication diary, you make a list of each pill you are taking and the time you are supposed to take it. Place a tick next to each pill as you take it.
- Keep track of your medication supply and prepare for holidays, weekends, and other times when you might not be able to get immediate refills.
- Be honest with your doctor about any problems you have with adherence.
- Use timers or your mobile phone to remind you when to take your dose. Reliable friends and family can also help.
- Keep a day's worth of emergency medicine with you at all times.

Summing Up

- Common side affects of HIV medicines can be reduced and made bearable through therapeutic remedies or through treatment adjustments. While side effects should be reported to your doctor, especially if they become bothersome, you can manage most of these on your own.

- Long-term side effects can be managed through therapeutic remedies or other medicines. A doctor must be closely involved in managing long-term side effects.

- Worrisome side effects are dangerous and should be reported to your doctor immediately. These effects can be life-threatening if you do not take care of them immediately.

- Keep taking your medicine. Side effects can be managed by either changes in medicine or complementary techniques. If you wait until you are really sick to begin taking medicine, you will not do as well on the therapy.

- Blood tests are the way to keep ahead of what the HIV is doing. You need blood tests to make sure your body is responding to treatment and to tell you when to change treatment.

- IRIS is a syndrome that occurs when your immune system is restarted. Although it usually goes away on its own it can become serious and life-threatening.

- Drugs interact with each other and with over-the-counter medicines, herbs, street drugs, alternative medicines, and even with caffeine and alcohol. Make sure you keep a list of all your medicines and habits so that your physicians can help avoid negative interactions.

- Once you start to take medicine for AIDS you should not stop. Adherence is the best policy. Experimental structured treatment interruption has not had positive results as of yet.

Chapter Six

What Infections are Dangerous to HIV/AIDS Patients?

What is an opportunistic infection?

An opportunist infection is a disease that the immune system normally blocks without much effort. For example, when you take a walk, you do not normally pay much attention to the bugs around you; you ignore them if they're not bothersome. This is how your immune system treats many diseases: they are not really a big problem, and so it ignores them. However, AIDS works like a horror movie and makes a little problem big. It shrinks your immune system down to the size of the minor diseases. These diseases then take advantage of your reduced system.

Having AIDS can lower your immune system's ability to fight disease. Since any disease, from colds to chickenpox, can devastate your body, some diseases attack as your CD4 count drops.

'An opportunist infection is a disease that the immune system normally blocks without much effort.'

Opportunistic Infections

CD4 Count	Disease	Affects	Agent
500 cells/mm³ – 200 cells/mm³	Thrush (candidiasis)	Mouth/vagina	Fungus
	Kaposi's sarcoma	Body/internal organs	Virus
200 cells/mm³ – 100 cells/mm³	Pneumocystis carinii pneumonia (PCP)	Lungs	Fungus
	Histoplasmosis	Body	Fungus
	Coccidioidomycosis	Body	Fungus
	Progressive multifocal leukoencephalopathy (PML)	Brain	Virus
100 cells/mm³ – 50 cells/mm³	Toxoplasmosis	Brain	Parasite
	Cryptosporidiosis	Intestines	Protozoa
	Cryptococcosis	Brain (and the rest of the body)	Fungus
	Cytomegalovirus (CMV)	Eyes and intestines	Virus
Less than 50 cells/mm³	Mycobacterium avium complex (MAC)	Lungs, intestines, blood	Bacteria

Treatment in advance

In order to prevent opportunistic infections from getting a foothold in your body, your doctor may determine it is best to treat you for them in advance. Before HIV turns into AIDS, you should be vaccinated against many infectious diseases if your doctor feels that would be safe for you. It is also a good idea to have a tuberculosis test and undergo treatment if there is any chance you are carrying the disease. However, there are some opportunistic infections without vaccines because they are normally not a problem for people.

Waiting until you have an opportunistic infection may be too late to treat it. Many times people with AIDS suffer with multiple infections at the same time. Opportunistic infections are also involved in the onset of IRIS. The medicines you are prescribed will keep you healthier longer, so it is important to take them.

Are people with HIV more prone to cancer?

People with HIV have a much higher risk of cancer because their immune system is weak and cannot take care of cancer cells before they spread. People with HIV are also more likely to be infected with viruses that cause cancer such as human herpes virus 8 (HHV8), Epstein-Barr virus (EBV), human papillomavirus (HPV), and hepatitis B virus (HBV).

There are some common cancers such as breast cancer, prostate cancer and colorectal cancer that carry the same risks for HIV-positive and HIV-negative individuals. However, there are other cancers that have such a high risk for AIDS patients that they are often called 'AIDS defining cancers': Kaposi's sarcoma, non-Hodgkin's lymphoma (AIDS-related lymphoma), and invasive cervical cancer. Cancers that AIDS patients are more susceptible to acquiring are: anal cancer, cervical cancer, Hodgkin's lymphoma, liver cancer and lung cancer.

Although HIV is responsible for the increased risk of cancer, there are certain risky trends such as smoking and heavy alcohol use that can increase your risk by even greater numbers. If you are HIV-positive, reduce as many as you can of the cancer risk factors you can control. Women should be screened regularly for cancer with a Pap smear. It is also possible for men who have had sex with other men to be screened with an anal Pap smear to detect and treat early signs of anal cancer.

'Waiting until you have an opportunistic infection may be too late to treat it.'

How are MAC and TB related?

Both MAC (mycobacterium avium complex) and TB (tuberculosis) are caused by bacteria in the mycobacterium family. MAC is present everywhere and almost everyone carries it in their bodies, but it only makes people sick when their immune systems are weak. TB is a respiratory disease that has active and latent stages. When a person contracts TB, they must stay on the medicine for around six to nine months in order to get rid of it. People who stop taking medicine early will continue to carry TB in the latent phase in their bodies. Having a weak immune system can cause latent TB to become active.

'Although HIV is responsible for the increased risk of cancer, there are certain risky trends such as smoking and heavy alcohol use that can increase your risk by even greater numbers.'

MAC is a disease that affects the blood. Symptoms are diarrhoea, abdominal pain, fever, fatigue and night sweats. When a person's CD4 count drops close to 50, their healthcare providers may want them to take prophylaxis (preventative medicine) to keep MAC from attacking their system. If a person with HIV is carrying MAC that has been confirmed through a blood or tissue culture, he or she will need to be on antibiotics for the rest of their life. Like TB it is difficult to get rid of MAC.

A person who has had TB at any time in their life will test positive on a TB skin test. If your skin test is positive, you may have to have an X-ray to determine whether or not the TB is latent or no longer inside your body. Some doctors may place you on a course of TB medicine for nine months just to be safe. Active TB is highly contagious and spreads through the air. The symptoms of TB are coughing up blood, weight loss, fever and night sweats. People with active TB may need to be isolated from other people or hospitalised for a few weeks until the medicine begins to work.

Is pneumonia associated with HIV/AIDS?

There are several types of pneumonia, and those who are HIV-positive are susceptible to them all. However, one type of pneumonia, pneumocystis carinii pneumonia (PCP), is characteristic of only AIDS-infected people. This type of pneumonia lives inside many people, but it does not affect them at all. People who are HIV-positive and do not get treatment for this type of pneumonia will begin to cough and have chest pain. As the disease progresses less and less oxygen gets into the blood, and the patient can die.

Preventing hypochondria

With all the different symptoms and diseases a person with HIV can contract, it is easy to think that you must have all the diseases associated with AIDS. Please keep in mind that as long as you adhere to your treatment and are diagnosed early, you can live an almost normal lifespan.

To prevent yourself from becoming a hypochondriac, there are several steps you can take. First, you must find a trusted relative or friend who will come to the doctor with you. Then, ask your doctor to help you prioritise your symptoms. With their help, make a list of which symptoms need immediate attention.

Next, get a journal. At the top of each journal entry make a list of any symptoms you have that day and write down their times. At the bottom of the page, keep track of feelings, thoughts and emotions you had about how you felt that day. When you are finished writing in your journal, tell yourself that you are not a doctor and cannot diagnose your symptoms. Then, if you are concerned about your symptoms for that day, share your journal with your friend. Your friend should have a copy of the list of important symptoms that tells you when you should contact your doctor immediately. Let your friend help you decide if any of your symptoms are important enough to make a trip to the doctor.

'Do not let your fears of becoming sick control you.'

If your symptoms are not urgent, you can take your diary to the doctor with you on your next visit and discuss them with him or her. If you decide your symptoms are urgent, go to the doctor as instructed. Do not let your fears of becoming sick control you. Find a mental health specialist to talk to about your fears. Joining a support group with people who are going through the same trouble as you, will also be very helpful.

Summing Up

- Opportunistic infections are infections that are normally harmless to healthy adults. When your immune system is weakened, they step in and attack in full force.

- Some doctors take a proactive stance against opportunistic infections. These doctors prefer to fight the infections before you get them and may give you antibiotics in advance. Take any medicines your doctor gives you as prescribed.

- People with HIV have an increased amount of risk for certain types of cancers. Some of these cancers occur so much more frequently in patients with AIDS, they are considered to be 'AIDS defining cancers'.

- MAC and TB are two common opportunistic infections that are related bacteria. TB can remain latent in the body for years and show up when your immune system weakens. TB is deadly when active. MAC is found everywhere and does not generally cause a problem unless a person's immune system is severely suppressed. Once MAC is active, it wreaks havoc on the body and can kill.

- Pneumocystis carinii pneumonia (PCP) is a type of pneumonia that infects many adults without causing any symptoms. In HIV-positive individuals, it can be deadly.

- With all the different opportunistic infections HIV-positive people can incur, it is difficult to not become a hypochondriac and run to the doctor with every new symptom. Keep track of your symptoms, but do not worry about them. Talk them over with a friend and your doctor. Join a support group, and find a mental health specialist with whom to share your fears.

Chapter Seven

Keeping Well

Eat healthy

Eating healthy for a HIV-positive person involves two things: eating appetising and nutritious foods and preparing foods safely so they will not cause an infection. In order to prepare safe food to eat, follow these guidelines:

- Always wash your hands before preparing food, after handling raw meat, and before eating anything.

- Use stainless steel, porcelain and plastic utensils/surfaces. Throw out or replace wooden ones. Use clean utensils and dishes for all the foods you prepare. Anything that touches raw meat should be washed before touching anything else.

- Cook meats, fish, seafood and eggs until they are all the way done. Do not eat partially cooked foods.

- Only choose hard, pasteurised cheeses to eat.

- Thaw frozen items in the refrigerator.

- Sanitise surfaces with bleach water.

- If there is a little mould on your bread, toss the whole loaf. Store bread in the freezer and get it out as needed in order to preserve it longer.

- Keep an eye on things that expire and toss them when they reach their expirations.

In brief, the foods you should eat are:

- Small servings of foods that are high in energy.

- High-protein foods.

'Eating healthy for a HIV-positive person involves two things: eating appetising and nutritious foods and preparing foods safely so they will not cause an infection.'

- Supplemental vitamins and minerals.

- Foods that appear appetising on your plate and smell enticing. Some AIDS patients may need more flavouring so they can taste it; others may prefer no flavouring because it upsets their mouth or stomach.

- If you get sick of eating, start thinking of eating as being your job. It is your way of fighting against the virus that is trying to take over your body.

- If you regularly consume more than five alcoholic beverages per day, consider seeking help to reduce your alcohol intake. Alcohol provides empty calories that can make you feel full without offering nutritional value.

When you go out to eat, at home or on holiday, be careful where you eat. Choose restaurants that:

'Treatment failure is when the drug regimen you are taking stops working.'

- Have good reputations and good records for cleanliness. Search online to find reviews, news reports and surveys to see what other people thought about them.

- Choose safe foods to eat like pizza, breads, and fruits and vegetables that you can peel before eating.

- Do not go to a restaurant that keeps food under heat lamps.

- Choose an upscale restaurant.

- Make sure the food is hot when served, and well cooked.

- Never buy food from a street vendor.

- Drink only bottled water and juices when out of the country. Wipe all caps before opening. Beer and wine are also safe beverages to drink.

- If you cannot find bottled water, you can boil water for three minutes to clean it.

Prevent treatment failure

Treatment failure is when the drug regimen you are taking stops working. Your CD4 count will begin to show a downward sloping trend while your viral load trend will slope upwards. There are three reasons for treatment failure. Virologic failure is when the medicines stop lowering the amount of virus in your blood.

Immunologic failure is when the immune system stops responding to the medicines you were prescribed. Clinical progression is when a person is taking the medications but shows symptoms of AIDS.

Some risk factors that contribute to treatment failure are:

- Neglecting to take your prescribed medication. Taking your medicine and adhering to your timetable is of vital importance. This cannot be stressed enough. Take all the pills your doctor prescribes, and take them on time.

- Drug resistance.

- Your body does not absorb the medication well.

- Previous treatment failure.

- Illnesses or other conditions.

- Substance abuse in combination with poor adherence.

- Beginning treatments when you are in poor health.

- Side effects or interactions from medications.

Keep a list of all medicines, alternative medicines, any illegal substances and other drugs you are taking and have taken. Include the name of the medication, when you started it, when you stopped it (if this applies) who prescribed it, what your dose was, what side effects you had, and why you were on the drug. Take your list with you to all your doctor appointments and any appointments with alternative medicine providers. This record can help support all the information the doctors have.

Do not take recreational drugs

Drugs use is common among AIDS patients. Some people become AIDS patients because they shared a needle while taking recreational drugs. Some AIDS patients turn to illegal drugs when their medicines are not working properly or the side effects are unbearable. Illegal drugs should be avoided because they are difficult to regulate and they can cause harmful interactions with your medicine routine.

'Illegal drugs should be avoided because they are difficult to regulate and they can cause harmful interactions with your medicine routine.'

There are several reasons to not take illegal drugs, but one of the major reasons involves risk. When a person takes illegal drugs, they act in ways that are risky to themselves. They are more inclined to share needles. They are more inclined to have unprotected sex. If you have unprotected sex with another HIV-positive person, you could create a resistant form of HIV. If you have unprotected sex with a HIV-negative person, you could infect them.

One final negative about taking drugs while on HIV medications: people who are taking illegal drugs tend to forget to take their medicines or sleep through the times to take their medicines. This can ruin the outcome of your prognosis and create resistant HIV, making it difficult to lower your viral load.

Quit smoking

People who are HIV-positive increase their risk of being sick and of contracting cancers. People who smoke increase these cancer risks and increase the risks of becoming sick in general. Instead of piling two high risk factors on top of each other, try to quit smoking.

Here are some tips if you want to quit:

- Ask family and friends to not smoke around you.

- Find a good mental health specialist to help reduce stress in your life.

- Talk to your doctor about treatments that help people to stop smoking.

- Recognise routines that compel you to smoke and find something else to do with your hands during the times you would traditionally light up. Knitting, mosaics, and sculpture are good examples of what you could do to keep them busy.

- During this time, chew sugar-free gum to keep your mouth busy as well.

- Consider other alternative stress-relieving therapies such as massage therapy, acupuncture, or meditation.

For more information, see *Stop Smoking: The Essential Guide* (Need2Know).

Do not share your HIV with others. Do not let others share their illnesses with you

There are several day-to-day things we do that can increase the chances of sharing HIV with another individual. They also can increase your chances of another person sharing their diseases with you. If you are HIV-positive, please:

- Do not share your toothbrush.
- Do not share your razor.
- Do use condoms.
- Stay away from people who are sick. Even diseases that do not normally make other people sick can make you sick.
- Do not share fingernail or cuticle scissors.
- Do not share pierced jewellery that may have blood on it.

Take care of your mental health

HIV not only drains your body, it also drains your mind. It is common for people with HIV to become depressed even when they have a good prognosis. Fight depression before it starts by finding a highly reputable mental health provider as soon as you are diagnosed. Here are some other tips for maintaining your mental health:

- Join a support group.
- Find a hobby you enjoy and stick with it.
- Eat smaller, healthier meals.
- Talk about your feelings and fears with your doctor or a close friend.
- Get enough sleep (at least eight hours each night).

If you begin to lack motivation to do anything throughout the day, or if you only want to sleep all the time, or if you find yourself having angry outbreaks or weeping spells you cannot control, seek help immediately. You do not have to live in a dark cloud.

'HIV not only drains your body, it also drains your mind.'

Exercise

Exercise is an important part of any wellness plan. To make it truly beneficial you should try to do exercise at least three times per week. Some doctors recommend a mixed routine of exercise for your heart and lungs, exercise for your muscles and exercise to relieve stress. Talk to your doctor about what kinds of exercise would be good for you and how frequently, and how long you should do exercise. Although it might seem counterproductive, people who are feeling tired and begin an exercise routine tend to get more energy. Be sure to stretch when you exercise to prevent injury.

Exercise offers these benefits:

- Helps control side effects like high blood sugar and increased blood fats
- Increases muscle mass
- Reduces the fat from the stomach area
- Reduces stress
- Gives you more energy
- Strengthens your bones

Exercises for the heart and lungs:

- Climbing stairs
- Walking
- Cycling

Exercises to build muscle:

- Sit-ups
- Push-ups
- Lifting light weights (less than five pounds)
- Chin-ups

Exercises to help you relieve stress:

- Tai chi

* Martial arts

* Yoga

Find a support group

There are many support groups out there. Some are for people with HIV in general, some are for people with AIDS, some are for adults and some are for children. Ask around, use the resources in the back of this book, go online and find a group that meets your needs for companionship. If you want, you can even try several groups to find one that is a good fit.

There are support groups for friends and family. Take someone along with you to make the introduction to the group easier.

Summing Up

- It is very important to maintain a healthy diet. It is equally important to eat foods that have not been contaminated with things that could make you sick. Keep your kitchen clean, and only eat at restaurants that have a reputation for cleanliness.

- Treatment failure is when your medication stops working. You can prevent treatment failure by sticking to your medicine regimen.

- Taking drugs is not only bad for your body, but it increases your chances of participating in risky behaviours. If you have a drug problem, get help.

- Smoking also increases your risks for disease and cancers. Try to quit smoking if you can.

- Do not share diseases. Do not risk infecting others by not allowing them to use items that may have your blood on them. Keep yourself from getting other's diseases by staying away from them and items that may carry their germs when they are sick.

- Find a reputable mental health provider to take care of your mental health needs. Treat your mental health before it becomes an issue.

- Exercise can give your immune system and your emotions a boost. Ask your doctor about the types of exercise you should do.

- There are many support groups for people with HIV and their friends and family members. Find one that meets your needs.

Chapter Eight

What to do When a Friend or Family Member is Diagnosed with HIV/AIDS

Be supportive

The best thing you can do for any friend or loved one in a time of distress is to be supportive. Being supportive does not mean coming up with a million ideas that will help fix their problem, it means listening. Allow them to discuss their fears with you.

You can touch and hug people who are HIV-positive without contracting the disease, if you were used to touching and hugging your friend or family member, continue to do so.

Spend time together, watch the TV, get a group of friends together for an informal gathering, or go and see a film.

If you are sick, stay away from any person who is HIV-positive. They are much more prone to contracting infections and diseases. You can still post cards, email or ring them. Because he or she is at an elevated risk for infection, make sure to cover any wounds you have before visiting. It is important to wash your hands frequently: after using the toilet, before preparing food, after using a tissue, etc.

'The best thing you can do for any friend or loved one in a time of distress is to be supportive.'

Watch for signs of depression and get them help if they need it

When anyone is faced with a diagnosis like HIV or AIDS, there are four very natural responses: denial, anger, anxiety and fear. Although these are not always the best way to respond to a problem, they are standard ways of working through things.

Denial

Signs of denial:

- Avoiding uncomfortable activities such as talking about HIV or AIDS and the diagnosis.
- Refusing to admit he or she has the disease.
- Misinterpreting what is really happening, what other people are saying and what other people are doing.
- Making excuses or lying about why he or she is doing something or not doing something.

Denial is one way some people use to deal with difficult situations. It can work well as long as it is used as a coping strategy and not as a crutch. If your friend or family member remains in denial for a long period of time, you should talk to their healthcare provider. Denial can make treatments more difficult and ineffective sooner.

Anger

Anger is another management strategy. Here are some signs of anger:

- Tension
- Elevated blood pressure
- Frown or angry face
- Acts of aggression

- Elevated heart rate
- Agitation
- Body language

Anger may be the first feeling a person goes through when they discover they have HIV or AIDS, or they may display signs of denial first. Anger directed at the HIV can make a person ready to stand up and fight. It can energise the HIV patient to action. However, anger also has a bad side. Anger can cause people to lash out or hurt loved ones. Anger can cause big explosions over small events. If you think that your friend or loved one has developed an unhealthy anger response to cope with his or her diagnosis, contact professional mental health help. Never allow someone to hurt you physically or blame you for his or her problems. Realise that anger harmfully directed like that needs to be harnessed and the underlying problems need to be resolved.

Fear

Fear is another coping strategy and here are some of its signs:

- Dilated pupils
- Tense muscles
- Lack of focus
- Elevated heart rate and blood pressure

Fear is an emotion related to anger. Both of them have similar signs. Fear is a normal feeling, but sometimes it can take over a person's life. If you believe your friend or loved one is allowing his or her fear to consume them, get the help of a mental health professional.

Anxiety

Anxiety is one of the more common coping strategies. Here are some signs of it:

- Racing heart
- Sweating

'Anger directed at the HIV can make a person ready to stand up and fight.'

- Nervousness
- Shortness of breath
- Trouble sleeping
- Trouble concentrating
- Dizziness or feeling faint
- Headaches and muscle tension
- Restlessness

Although anxiety is another normal reaction to discovering you are HIV-positive or have contracted AIDS, it is important that the anxiety does not prevent you from doing normal activities. Anxiety can lead to depression. Seek medical advice if your friend or family member develops severe anxiety.

Depression

Depression is not normal and needs to be taken care of immediately by a mental healthcare professional. Depression will not go away on its own. If you notice the signs of depression in you, your friend or a family member who has been diagnosed with HIV or AIDS, get help immediately.

Signs of depression:

- Difficulty focusing or concentrating
- Trouble sleeping
- Fatigue
- Negative feelings about and directed towards self
- Not interested in things that normally would excite or interest the person
- Changes in appetite or weight
- Suicidal thoughts

Dealing with a sick person you care about can be a difficult task. People with AIDS or any terminal illness may have periods of time where it seems like they are going to die. Then, they make a miraculous recovery. These times cycle back and forth and can be very draining on those who support them. If you are finding it difficult to deal with the strain, seek the help of a healthcare or mental healthcare professional.

Another poor way to work through problems is by turning to drugs or alcohol. These are not healthy ways of dealing with stress. Talk to a doctor or mental health provider if you are concerned about yours, or your friend or loved one's drugs or alcohol abuse.

Help them stick to a healthy diet

Sometimes people with HIV lose interest in food. They may be too tired to prepare food on their own. Following the guidelines in chapter 7, you can prepare a meal for your friend. Do not expect him or her to eat a six-course meal, but something small, colourful and appealing will be appreciated.

Never prepare a meal or handle food it you have diarrhoea. Many people do not realise how serious diarrhoea is, and how easily it is passed from one person to another. No matter how frequently you wash your hands or how clean you think you are, stay out of the kitchen when you have this malady.

You can also do research on the restaurants in your town to find ones that would be good to go to with your friend.

Exercise together

Exercise is a difficult thing to begin doing on your own. Exercise is very helpful for those who have HIV. However, sometimes, people with HIV are not interested in exercising because they feel fatigued. You can show them you care by encouraging them to go on walks with you.

Find a shop they like to visit and walk to it. Perhaps the shop sells pre-packaged sweets or biscuits. If they enjoy eating these foods, you could get some and eat them together. Or perhaps they prefer to look through knick-knacks. Walk to the nearest shop and browse with them. Find something that motivates them or at least will give them a little incentive to go. Keep each trip short so they are interested in going again.

Set up a routine that will not interfere with their medicine timetable or any naps they may need to take. Then stick to it so they have something to look forward to each day.

Go to the doctor together

People with HIV have many things on their minds. Going to a doctor with them can help relieve some of the stress. Take a notebook and keep notes of the appointment for them. Write down the answers to any questions that they ask. Help them remember to take their list of medications, their side effects journal, and their medication record.

If you know they wanted to ask the doctor questions about a specific topic, help remind them of it before going into the office.

You may also need to encourage your friend or family member to take their medicines or to go to appointments. You can help them determine which side effects are serious and which are not, unless you tend to be a bit of a hypochondriac yourself. If that is the case, have the foresight to find someone else for that job.

Be an advocate for your friend or family member. Learn as much as you can about HIV and AIDS. Use your knowledge to reassure and encourage your loved one.

While you are taking your friend to the doctor, be sure to get check-ups and vaccinations for yourself as well. You need to stay in good health in order to be a solid support for your friend or family member.

'Be an advocate for your friend or family member. Learn as much as you can about HIV and AIDS. Use your knowledge to reassure and encourage your loved one.'

Join a support group

There are support groups that you can join with your friend, but you should also consider finding a support network for yourself as well. Friends of people with HIV or AIDS have their own challenges and daily struggles. They also have to overcome prejudice and discrimination frequently without specific laws protecting them.

You and your family member or friend can also celebrate World AIDS Day, which is 1st December. There are events around the world on this day. You can check out their website at www.worldaidsday.org.

Honour a memory

If you have lost a friend or loved one to HIV, there are plenty of ways to honour him or her. You can attend or host an International Candlelight Memorial. See the website www.candlelightmemorial.org.

You can create a collage or a quilt with memories of your friend or loved one. Gather scraps of cloth or pictures and a frame and piece it together.

You can volunteer for any of the local AIDS support groups or educational agencies. This is a great way to get more information to people about HIV and AIDS.

Summing Up

- People diagnosed with HIV need friends and support throughout their condition. You can organise outings and informal parties, or you can just spend time with them. Try to keep their lives as normal as possible.

- Watch your friend or family member for signs of depression and other signs that they might not be handling the situation well. If you notice worrisome traits in your friend or in yourself, speak with a mental health professional about them.

- Encourage your friend to eat, and cook meals for your friend when you can. No one should cook if they are experiencing diarrhoea because it is a highly contagious condition.

- Get out with your friend. Find a unique place to walk to each day and take your friend for a treat. Exercising in moderation and under the advice of a physician is healthy and can be fun.

- Go with your family member or friend to the doctor. Help him or her keep track of any questions and the answers to the questions. Help determine which side-effects are normal and which need immediate attention.

- Join a support group with your friend and find one for yourself as well. Dealing with the ups and downs of a terminal illness can wear on you. Find something that will return your energy to you.

- Honour the memory of a friend or family member you've lost to AIDS. Start a candlelight memorial or volunteer with a local organisation. Create a collage or even a quilt filled with the memories of your loved one.

Chapter Nine

Making the Most of Life After a HIV/ AIDS Diagnosis

Dealing with discrimination

The 2005 version of the Disability Discrimination Act (DDA) prohibits discrimination in the workplace within the United Kingdom. It was strengthened by the Equality Act in 2010 and includes people who are HIV-positive. This act prevents someone from discriminating against you in trade union membership, in education, in accommodation and other housing issues like letting and selling property, in your ability to get goods and services, and in employment.

At work, you have a legal right to not tell anyone that you are HIV-positive. If your employer requires testing or disclosure as a part of the job, he or she must require everyone to have the same testing or fill out the same forms. Your employer is not allowed to sack you because he or she discovers your HIV status. An employer also cannot use your HIV status when determining whether or not to hire you.

The UK Data Protection Act 1998 allows you to keep any personal details, including those about the status of your health, private. No one is able to use your personal information or give it away unless you have given him or her authorisation to do so.

'No one is able to use your personal information or give it away unless you have given him or her authorisation to do so.'

If you are a victim of a crime because of your HIV status, it will lead to stronger sentences for the perpetrators because the courts will consider it an aggravating factor.

Dealing with people's preconceptions of HIV/AIDS

There will always be ignorant people in this world. There will also always be people who disagree with you on certain topics. And, unfortunately, it seems it is human nature to develop preconceived notions about certain people. No one is immune from this flaw.

'The more you can teach another person about your condition, the more likely they will be to accept it.'

However, the best way to change the minds of the general population is to let them see who you are. You can compel people to follow rules with the threat of lawsuits and police enforcement, but the hate and the preconceptions will not stop until you show them that you do not live up to that stereotype they have of you. Use your actions, like working hard, to show them you cannot be placed into the box they designed for you.

Studies performed by NAT show a link between prejudice and ignorance. If these studies were performed worldwide, the same trends would appear. The more you can teach another person about your condition, the more likely they will be to accept it. Use this book and government resources to reinforce your voice.

There are laws in place to protect you if you are HIV-positive, so you do not have to hide, and in some cases, you might not be able to hide. The change has to start with you treating your disease as if it is something anyone could have, like a cold or a broken bone. Then, you have to inform people about it. Teach them about HIV. Let them know that they should get tested, too, because you did not think it would happen to you either.

Travelling with HIV/AIDS

People who are HIV-positive can still travel if certain precautions are taken. If you want to travel outside the United Kingdom, keep in mind that most Asian countries, Australia, Canada, Central America, the Middle East, and some countries in South America, Eastern Europe and Africa will not allow confirmed HIV-positive or people suspected of being HIV-positive into the country. You can visit this website to get up-to-date information about the restrictions specific countries place on people travelling with HIV: www.hivtravel.org.

If you are travelling internationally, you should probably not travel to Third World countries, for your own safety. Sanitation standards are often not safe for people with HIV.

Talk to you doctor and see if he or she can recommend a HIV doctor who practises in the area where you are travelling. Plan in advance for any setbacks that might occur by taking a week's supply of antibiotics in case you get traveller's diarrhoea. Be sure that you will have a way of covering any medical costs while you travel.

Try to keep a barrier between you and any animal faeces or animals that you meet. Wear shoes and put towels down on benches, sand, and soil before sitting. Take all your prescribed medications on your regular schedule.

Swimming is always risky for those with HIV. Water is the ideal carrier for a variety of disease-causing agents. It is best to stay out of the water and enjoy the beach.

'Swimming is always risky for those with HIV.'

When eating on holiday, you should still research the restaurants you are planning to eat at as much as possible. Stick to any diets that your doctor has prescribed for you. Remember to wash and then peel any fruits or vegetables and avoid those that you cannot peel. Have your food well cooked and do not order meat if you cannot get it prepared that way. Stick with bottled water and bottled juices. Never buy food from a street vendor.

Do I need to get rid of my pet?

Because your immune system is compromised, and pets carry diseases, you may feel like you need to give up your pet. While this a choice only you can make, keep in mind that pets provide unbiased companionship and have been shown to be beneficial for AIDS patients as long as certain precautions are followed.

The most common diseases AIDS patients get from their pets are toxoplasmosis, cryptosporidiosis and MAC. There are other diseases you can get from your pet as well, so take as many precautions as you can around it.

Always wash your hands after handling a pet and before eating or cooking. You cannot give HIV to your pet.

If you have decided to get a new pet, get an older cat or dog. Kittens and puppies are especially prone to infectious diarrhoea and playful nipping and scratching. Do not handle any pets with diarrhoea and have someone else take them to the vets for you if possible. Keep your animals inside as much as possible so that they do not eat other animals or the faeces of other animals. Do not touch or take in stray animals.

Feed your pet only pet food that was designed for it. If your pet eats undercooked or uncooked meat, it can transfer any infectious material to you. Do not allow your pet to scratch you. If you are scratched or bitten, you need to wash the area immediately, and you may need to seek medical advice.

If you have a dog, do not clean up its faeces. If you have a cat, do not change its litter tray. If you do not have anyone else to do it, you will need to learn how to put on and take off disposable gloves properly. Wear them each time you pick up after your dog, or change the litter tray, and then throw them away and wash your hands afterwards. Birds and fish are also acceptable pets, but use the same precautions when cleaning cages or aquariums. Avoid other exotic pets and reptiles.

Avoid kissing your pet, or allowing your pet to kiss you. Keep your pet free of fleas.

When you visit other people with pets, use the same precautions as you would for your own pet. Do not touch any animal that may be unhealthy. Avoid farm animals. They are constantly outside and exposed to many diseases that are easy for you to catch.

Supervise HIV-positive children carefully around pets. They have a tendency to want to cuddle, and the animal may scratch or bite to get away. Supervise them when they are washing their hands after dealing with an animal as well.

My partner was diagnosed as HIV-positive can we still have sex?

Having sex with a HIV-positive person is always a risk, even if you are both HIV-positive. Whether or not you have sex with a HIV-positive person depends first on if you and your partner are willing to take any risk, and second on how much risk you feel able to take.

Initial studies performed to measure how well condoms prevent the spread of HIV show that they are 90% effective at preventing the transmission of HIV. Currently, the condom is the most recommended way of preventing the transmission of HIV from one person to another.

There have also been some preliminary studies done in Switzerland that show when HIV is controlled by drug therapy there is little chance of transmission of HIV between two unprotected partners. These tests were done on monogamous couples. In these tests, the infected person had a viral load below 40 over the past six months because of medical treatment. However, the point was noted that past viral load does not predict future viral load. Also having an STI can permit HIV to be transmitted even under these conditions.

How you have sex is another factor to consider. Anal sex is the easiest way to transmit HIV. Vaginal and oral sex will still transmit the virus, but the risk is slightly lower.

If you and your partner feel comfortable with the risks you can continue to have sex. If one of you is uncomfortable with the situation, it is probably best if you do not have sex. There are other methods of sharing with your partner, from massage to mutual masturbation that allow you to remain close without actually having sex.

'Initial studies performed to measure how well condoms prevent the spread of HIV show that they are 90% effective at preventing the transmission of HIV.'

Sex after HIV/AIDS

If you are HIV-positive and you want to continue having sex, there are several things you must do to prevent the spread of HIV. There are also several ethical concerns you should consider. The first is that you should always stick to your drug regimen. The studies carried out in Switzerland showed people with no detectable HIV in their bloodstream had a much lower chance of transmitting the virus to others, even through sexual contact, as long as there were no other STIs or open wounds. Use your medical treatment as your first line of defense.

Tell your partner that you have HIV. HIV at worst kills and at best impairs a person for life. Telling someone you are HIV-positive before having sex with them and allowing them to make the decision about whether or not to proceed, shows you respect them and their rights.

There is a chance if you tell the person, they will not want to have sex with you at all and your relationship will change or end, but there is also a chance they will not have a problem with the relationship. If you wait to tell the person until after the encounter, your relationship will change or end anyway because they may feel you have betrayed them and did not respect their right to choose.

'Telling someone you are HIV-positive before having sex with them and allowing them to make the decision about whether or not to proceed, shows you respect them and their rights.'

Even if you are having sex with another HIV-positive person, you should inform them of your status, use a condom, and stick to your medical treatment. If the form of the virus you have is different from the form of the virus your partner has, you risk creating a superinfection or re-infection between the two of you if you practise unprotected sex. A superinfection or re-infection is when one HIV-positive person becomes infected with a different HIV mutation. This can lead to the formation of even more HIV mutations if the two forms combine.

Having a baby after being diagnosed with HIV

Some people still have children after becoming HIV-positive. One way to have a baby after being diagnosed with HIV works if only the man has the disease. If the woman is HIV-negative, the man's sperm can be washed of the HIV and the woman can be artificially inseminated. However, this is a very costly method and at least once a woman has gotten HIV from it. Regular artificial insemination methods work extremely well because the collected sperm is screened for HIV when it is donated.

Another option is to adopt a baby. If both parents-to-be are HIV-positive this may be the most practical method. They could also consider other forms of reproductive technology such as surrogacy.

Using PrEP is a new option being tested for couples who want to have a baby naturally, but are concerned because one partner is HIV-positive and the other is not. If the woman is HIV-positive, and she is on medicine that has kept her viral load levels low for the previous six months, the chances of the man contracting HIV from her are low, so they could try to have a baby together. If both are positive and want to have a child together, they should both get on therapy and lower their viral loads before attempting to get pregnant. Once their viral loads are undetected for six months they can try to have a child. There is no research on these methods, so it is uncertain what the chances are for the child becoming HIV-positive.

I have HIV/AIDS. Why didn't the doctor test my baby for the disease when it was born?

Babies are born with immature non-functioning immune systems that do not begin to work until they are about two months old. It could take longer for the immune system to develop if the baby is premature. Because of this, the baby will not produce antibodies to test for at least a couple of months. After the baby is old enough, the doctor will perform the test.

Be reassured that if you adhered to your treatment plan, and your viral load was low throughout your pregnancy, you baby will probably not contract HIV. In studies on women who adhered to their treatment and delivered by C-section, the baby was only HIV-positive 1-5% of the time. If you do nothing, your baby has about a 40% chance of being HIV-positive according to recent research.

'Be reassured that if you adhered to your treatment plan, and your viral load was low throughout your pregnancy, you baby will probably not contract HIV.'

Can I give my baby HIV/AIDS if I breastfeed?

HIV can be transmitted from mother to child when the child is breastfed. In addition, it is uncertain how much of the virus passes through to the child. If you have a low viral load, your chances of transmitting HIV to your baby are less than 0.5%. If you choose to breastfeed, you will need to use HIV medicines to control your viral load that are acceptable for use in infants.

Choosing not to breastfeed can have consequences, too. As stated previously, the baby has no ability to form immunity during the first two months of its life. Normally, a mother's breast milk provides this immunity. If your HIV has an undetectable viral load, you and your doctor have it under control. If you continue taking the medicines to keep it controlled, you may end up providing your child with some level of immunity if you breastfeed.

In the end, there needs to be more research on this topic. Women with HIV are having children all around the world. Knowing what is best for your child is important.

Summing Up

- The United Kingdom has laws that prohibit discrimination based on HIV status. Get informed about these laws and know your rights concerning them.

- There will always be people that do not understand HIV and AIDS. Make it your job to better inform them.

- People with HIV can travel as long as they make special arrangements in advance and take special precautions. Some countries will not allow HIV-positive people or people suspected of being HIV-positive to enter them.

- People who are HIV-positive do not have to give up their pets, but they will have to take extra safety measures when they are dealing with them. If you are HIV-positive, try to find someone else to clean pet faecal material and cages. Be careful of animals you do not know, and stay away from farm animals.

- Whether or not an infected person and non-infected person have sex is determined by what level of risk they are comfortable taking. Never pressure your partner to do something he or she is uncomfortable doing. Over time, views about risk may change, but there are other alternatives to try as well.

- If you want to have sex after you have been diagnosed with HIV, use a condom and try to keep your viral load low.

- The same rules that apply for sex apply for having a baby after being diagnosed with HIV. Keep your viral levels low. With having a baby, there are other options available, such as adoption, that you and your partner might want to explore.

- Babies are born without a developed immune system. Do not expect a doctor to test your baby for HIV until after the immune system has had time to mature, even if you are HIV-positive.

- There have not been many studies on the risks versus benefits of breastfeeding after having a baby. Gather as much information from your doctor as you can so you are able to make an informed choice.

Chapter Ten

Frequently Asked Questions

I heard HIV does not cause AIDS. Is this true?

At this point in time, it is not fully understood how HIV turns into AIDS. Because the trigger is not known, some people believe that HIV does not cause AIDS. To support this conclusion, they point out that some people who have HIV never develop AIDS. However, HIV is not the only disease that does not affect people who carry it.

Consider 'Typhoid Mary'. Mary lived around the turn of the 20th century. Born in Northern Ireland, she was one of the first known carriers for typhoid fever that showed no symptoms. Unfortunately for the people who employed her, she also was a cook. She spread typhoid fever to everyone who ate the food she cooked, killing some of them. Despite the fact that the law did all they could to convince her she was carrying the disease, she would not give up her occupation. She finally had to be locked in isolation until her death. She never believed she was sick or the cause of other people's sickness.

Before HIV was discovered as a virus, it was hypothesised that an infectious agent was causing AIDS. There has always been a clearly traceable path from person to person through body fluids. Although it is true that everyone who carries the HIV in their body does not develop AIDS, it is equally true that every person who has AIDS also carries the HIV in their body.

People have been researching HIV and AIDS for more than 30 years now. After all that research, the only hypothesis that has stood the test of time is that HIV causes AIDS.

'Although it is true that everyone who carries the HIV in their body does not develop AIDS, it is equally true that every person who has AIDS also carries the HIV in their body.'

Did scientists create HIV?

The first samples of blood we have that contain the HIV are from 1959. One sample is from the United Kingdom and the other sample was taken from the Democratic Republic of the Congo. At that point in time, it would have required more technology than what was available even to the scientists in the United Kingdom in order to have created the virus. In fact, the scientists of the time did not realise that the blood contained the virus. It was not until more recent tests that this fact was found.

Despite this knowledge, many people like to believe there was a conspiracy to eliminate certain groups of people that centred on the creation of the AIDS virus. In part, this is because HIV targeted homosexuals, people living in poverty, minorities and drug users. If scientists had created it to control these populations, then they would have done humanity a disservice. Today, the disease affects children and women, the young and the old. It is not selective in who it infects.

'Many people like to believe there was a conspiracy to eliminate certain groups of people that centred on the creation of the AIDS virus.'

Is there a cure?

With modern combination therapy, it seems as if HIV has been cured. Many people show no viral load while they are on successful combination treatment. However, if these people take a break from treatment, their viral load springs up and their CD4 count drops.

Sometimes rumours start about natural cures for HIV. Although some natural supplements have been discovered that act like HIV medications, none of them have cured a person of a HIV infection.

If you look at it in perspective, the way we treat HIV is by blocking some of the processes your cells use to remain alive. Because some of your cells need to continue doing these processes, the HIV can find a way of maintaining low levels of successful production or at least hibernating.

There have been some promising results with some treatments. With all the avenues of research, a cure may be found in the future. Until that time, we must be happy with what we can do now.

Need2Know

My partner just tested negative for HIV, so I don't have it, right?

HIV is not transmitted every time a person has sex. Some people can even build a resistance to HIV during certain periods of their lives and then lose the resistance later. The test your partner took showed his or her status at the time of the test. It did not show anything about your status. You need to get yourself tested and keep track of your risky behaviours past and present, as well as the behaviours of your partner(s).

Getting tested together is the best way to check your status.

If you are not in a monogamous relationship, you should know the status of all your partners, and you should be tested more frequently than those in monogamous relationships.

How bad is it really?

We know HIV is deadly. But with the new medicines, lives are being prolonged. However, HIV medicines are very expensive. When HIV-positive people do not practise adherence, resistance develops and more drug mixtures are needed. The risk continues to rise as opportunistic infections take over.

Statistics show that people with HIV who are working will work the same number of days throughout the year as those who do not have the virus. But these numbers do not include those who have become depressed and discouraged. These are the patients who give up working when the regimen of drugs, work and their fatigue form too difficult of a mixture.

Taking care of sick people is not the worst part of the problem. The worst part of the problem is that people spread the disease without even knowing they have contracted it. People over the age of 50 seem to have little desire to think or worry about HIV and their status, yet 13% of the people who developed AIDS in 2010 were over the age of 50.

'The worst part of the problem is that people spread the disease without even knowing they have contracted it.'

The vicious cycle of infection must stop. HIV tests take a minimum amount of time. People at risk for developing a HIV infection can have multiple opportunities for being tested throughout the year. They need to be honest with themselves and get tested. We need to catch the disease before it has a chance to spread to others.

How can I prevent infecting other people?

The easiest ways to prevent yourself from infecting other people is to stop having sex with others and keep all open wounds covered. If you develop open wounds in or on your mouth refrain from kissing anyone until they heal. Clean up your blood if you get it on anything. Practise adherence to your treatment timetable and keep your viral load levels at an undetectable level.

If you are a woman who is pregnant, get treated and get your viral loads down to undetectable levels so you do not pass them on to your child. Have a C-section to reduce your risk of transmitting the virus during birth.

If you do not want to infect others who are not HIV-positive, but you are not worried about developing resistant viruses, you may follow all of the previously mentioned precautions but still have sex with other HIV-positive individuals. It is still recommended you use a condom during sex.

'The important thing in any relationship is that both couples agree and feel comfortable with the risks they take.'

While anyone with HIV is capable of preventing others from contracting the disease with 100% safety, most people with the disease and their partners are willing to live with some risk. For example, some couples have been together for many years when one is found to be HIV-positive. If both are willing to live with a 10% risk, they will continue having sex with condoms. If they are willing to run a little more risk, the infected person will practise adherence, keeping his or her levels below detection for six months and they will begin having unprotected sex. The important thing in any relationship is that both couples agree and feel comfortable with the risks they take.

When a person is single and infected, his or her choices will be different from those who are in a relationship and infected.

What are the 'red flags' that I need to watch out for to catch a HIV infection early?

There are a few different warning signs or 'red flags' that occur during the early stages of a HIV infection.

The most common symptoms associated with the primary HIV infection are:

- Fever
- Swollen glands
- Rash

Other symptoms are:

- Pain in the muscles or joints
- Diarrhoea
- Headache
- Nausea and vomiting
- Weight loss
- Thrush
- Enlarged spleen and liver
- Symptoms with the nervous system

What is salvage therapy?

When antiretroviral drugs were originally made available, it was thought that people should take one drug at a time until HIV became resistant to it, and then switch to another drug. It was believed that this would extend the use of the few antiretroviral drugs that were available. This approach was called 'monotherapy'.

Today, there are a wide variety of drugs to choose from, and monotherapy was shown to increase the ability of the virus to develop resistance. At this point in time, it is believed that two new drugs should always be introduced at once.

When a person works through all the available drugs, though, they must wait until a new drug is developed. They can also try to get into a clinical trial of a new drug and hope to be randomly chosen to receive the drug instead of the placebo. A clinical trial is when a drug is in the final stages of being tested to see if it can be used on patients. At this stage, the drug has undergone all other safety tests on animals and now needs to be tested on humans before the drug maker can put it on the market to sell to the general population. HIV-positive people interested in participating in clinical trials need to discuss the risks and benefits with their doctor. They should also research the trials and make sure they are reputable and scientifically sound.

Salvage therapy is a last option chance. When nothing else is working it is all that is left to try. The best way to avoid salvage therapy is to always adhere to your regimen.

'HIV-positive people interested in participating in clinical trials need to discuss the risks and benefits with their doctor.'

If you have exhausted your supply of potential new medicines, but you have a stable CD4 count and seem to be managing, you may end up in a holding regimen. This is a process of conserving drugs so that you can start with two new drugs at the same time as soon as another drug appears on the market.

Do I have to tell my employer?

You do not have to tell anyone you have HIV if you do not want to. However, an employer has the right to test their employees as long as they do not discriminate between them. This means that every employee must take the same type of tests or fill out the same type of paperwork.

Your employer is not allowed to discriminate against you if you do disclose information to him or her about your HIV status. You cannot be fired or have your application ignored because you are HIV-positive.

If you work in the healthcare profession and you are found to be HIV-positive by your employer, you may be asked to change positions from one that deals with open wounds to one that does not. This is the only legal time your employer can make you change your job because of your HIV status.

Summing Up

- More than thirty years of research are behind the hypothesis that HIV causes AIDS. People with HIV do not always have AIDS, but everyone with AIDS has HIV.

- At the time the virus emerged, scientists did not even have equipment to see it. They would not have been able to create it in a lab.

- Although modern therapies can keep HIV loads at undetectable levels, they cannot erase HIV from the system. Someday there may be a cure, but as of now there is not.

- Everyone should get tested for HIV. A partner's HIV test does not test your HIV status.

- Although medicine can keep HIV under control, many people do not get tested or do not think they need to be tested. Because of this, HIV is spreading. It requires relatively little effort to save major cost of care for people who have acquired the disease.

- There are ways to prevent infecting others. But some HIV-positive people and their partners are willing to accept some risk. The level of risk or the choice to not take any risk is up to you and your partner to decide.

- There are a few characteristic traits of HIV in its early stages. If you exhibit any of the symptoms and you have been exposed or been performing risky behaviours, you should get tested.

- Salvage therapy is only used when there are no other options for treatment. It is used because the virus inside you is resistant and several treatments have failed. To prevent the need for salvage therapy, adhere to your drug regimen.

- You are not required to tell your employer about your HIV status, but there are legal ways for them to find out what it is. You cannot be fired for your HIV-positive status, but you can be made to switch to a different position if you work in healthcare with open wounds.

Glossary

Acute stage of infection
This is the first stage of a HIV infection that is usually without symptoms.

Adherence
When a HIV patient faithfully follows his or her treatment regimen.

AIDS
Acronym for acquired immune deficiency syndrome. Disease that causes people infected with it to lose their ability to fight other diseases by damaging the immune system.

Anaemia
When the iron in a person's blood is lower than it should be.

Antibody
A protein made by B-lymphocytes to capture antigens on disease agents.

Antiretroviral drugs (ARVs)
These are medicines that are used to fight against retroviruses such as HIV. They work because of the ineffective job that reverse transcriptase does.

Antiretroviral therapy (ART)
Antiretroviral therapy, or ART, is the term used to describe the combination of drugs an AIDS patient takes for therapy.

Binding protein
A key-like finger on the outside of a cell that takes hold of nutrients and brings them into the cell.

B-lymphocyte
These are white blood cells that fight infections by making antibodies.

Candidiasis
A yeast infection. AIDS patients can have chronic yeast infections that move from their mouths into their esophagus.

CD4 cell
These are white blood cells that fight infection and have a CD4 binding protein on them.

CD4 count
The concentration of CD4 cells/mm^3 of blood. Used to determine how well your body is fighting HIV.

Class-sparing regimen
A method of treating HIV that involves not using one type of anti-HIV drug. For example, a doctor may not use protease inhibitors during treatment until all other treatments have failed.

Clinical trial
The final level of testing a drug, using humans, before putting it on the market to sell.

Co-infection
A co-infection is when a person is infected with more than one disease at any point in time.

Combination therapy
A HIV therapy that uses at least two different drugs at any given point in time. Currently this is thought to be the best way to treat HIV. Highly active antiretroviral therapy (HAART) is a form of combination therapy.

Cryptococcus
A disease that can cause meningitis (a fungal brain infection) in people with HIV.

Cryptosporidiosis
Diarrhoea caused by a protozoan that is most common throughout the world, but only severe in patients with a low immune system. Cryptosporidiois infects the small intestines.

Cytomegalovirus (CMV)
A disease that is common but only has symptoms in people with lowered immune systems. It can lead to blindness and death. It can also be transmitted from a mother to her unborn child resulting in a miscarriage, stillbirth, or birth defects.

DNA (deoxyribonucleic acid)
The set of directions that tell your cell what to do to stay alive.

Drug resistance
When a disease can continue reproducing even when there are drugs present to prevent it from reproducing.

ELISA (enzyme-linked immunosorbent assay) or EIA (enzyme immunoassay)
This is one of the early tests done to determine if a person is infected with HIV. It involves washing a solid that contains HIV with your blood, secondary antibodies, and a chemical that will make the secondary antibodies change colour.

Encephalopathy
Injury to the brain caused by an infection. Symptoms are an altered mental state, such as the inability to concentrate, involuntary movements or seizures.

Entry or fusion inhibitors
Drugs that are used to block the entry of the HIV into a cell. They work by attaching to the HIV or by attaching to the T-cell on the outside and keeping the HIV from attaching to the T-cell.

Gene
A gene is one instruction on the set of instructions contained in DNA. One gene usually makes one protein.

Gene therapy
The manipulation of the genes in a cell in an effort to cure a disease.

Genotypic assay
The process of looking at the genes of HIV in order to determine which drugs it can resist.

Hepatitis
This is an inflamed liver caused by an infection. It can cause an overall feeling of sickness, jaundice and loss of appetite.

Highly active antiretroviral therapy (HAART)
HAART is a form of combination therapy using three drugs from two classes of antiretroviral therapy in order to fight HIV.

HIV

Human immunodeficiency virus is a virus that attacks the immune system's T-cells and causes AIDS.

HPV

Human papillomavirus. An STI that can cause genital warts or be without symptoms.

Immune reconstitution inflammatory syndrome (IRIS)

Immune reconstitution inflammatory syndrome is a condition that occurs when the immune system makes an amazing recovery after beginning medicine and overreacts to any infections that are present.

Immunodeficiency

When the immune system is damaged and is not functioning like it should.

Incubation period

The time it takes from when a virus enters the body to when the body shows the first identifying symptoms of the virus.

Kaposi's sarcoma

A cancer caused by a virus that most commonly affects the skin with raised bumps that can be purple, brown, red or black. These bumps can also be in the mouth, stomach, intestines and throat.

Leishmaniasis

A protozoan spread through sandflies. It can cause skin ulcers, or it can affect your entire body system.

Leukoencephalopathy

Infection in the brain's white matter or inner parts of the brain.

Maintenance therapy

Using treatments to just keep a person in a stable state.

Microbicide

A future application for women to use that will kill any diseases, including HIV. These will be designed to be applied up to eight hours in advance of intercourse.

Monotherapy
Original method of treating HIV that used one drug at a time. This approach was thought to keep HIV from developing resistance to all the available drugs for the longest period of time. It has since been shown that combination therapy is more effective at preventing drug resistance.

Mycobacterium avium complex (MAC)
Infection related to tuberculosis that only attacks people with lowered immune systems.

Non-Hodgkin's lymphoma
A cancer of the blood that is not a Hodgkin's lymphoma. These cancers begin with lymphocytes and are usually caused by an infection.

Non-nucleoside reverse transcriptase inhibitor (NNRTI)
A non-nucleoside reverse transcriptase inhibitor is a drug class that attaches to reverse transcriptase. In this way it prevents it from attaching to the RNA and making DNA.

Nucleoside reverse transcriptase inhibitor (NRTI)
A nucleoside reverse transcriptase inhibitor is a drug class that acts as a stop piece for a DNA chain that reverse transcriptase is making. When reverse transcriptase uses an NRTI instead of a nucleoside, it cannot attach anything else to the DNA chain it is making.

Nucleoside
A building block for RNA.

Opportunistic infection
An infection that normally would not cause symptoms, but can kill people with damaged immune systems.

Pelvic inflammatory disease (PID)
A disease usually caused by an STI that can be without symptoms or cause pelvic pain and irregular menstruation or discharge.

Pneumocystis carinii pneumonia (PCP)
An opportunistic infection that is characteristic of HIV. It can be found in many people but it does not have any symptoms associated with it because healthy immune systems suppress it well. It attacks the lungs and forms a pneumonia that can be deadly in AIDS patients.

Post-exposure prophylaxis (PEP)
Using antiretroviral therapy drugs to prevent HIV transmission after a HIV-negative person has been exposed to HIV.

Pre-exposure prophylaxis (PrEP)
Using antiretroviral therapy drugs to prevent HIV transmission before a HIV-negative person anticipates he or she will be exposed to HIV.

Protease inhibitor
A protein tool that has the job of cutting other proteins in the cell to shape them so they will work.

Rapid test
A HIV test that uses saliva or blood to determine HIV status within 20 minutes.

Retrovirus
A virus that is made from RNA and must be turned into DNA before it can reproduce.

Reverse transcriptase
A protein tool that turns RNA into DNA.

Ribonucleic acid (RNA)
A type of genetic material containing working genes, which are the directions that tell a cell what it needs to do. This is the only genetic material found inside a HIV.

Salvage therapy
A last resort therapy used only when HIV has shown drug resistance with multiple drugs and is no longer responding to regular treatment.

Septicaemia
Blood poisoning.

Seroconversion
The point when your body begins to make an antibody to fight a disease.

Sero-discordant
When a HIV-positive person is in a relationship with a HIV-negative person.

Superinfection or re-infection
When a HIV-positive person is infected with a second, different strain of HIV by another HIV-positive person.

T-cell
These are white blood cells that fight infection and have a CD4 binding protein on them.

Therapeutic HIV vaccine
A HIV vaccine that is given to HIV-positive people to extend treatment without adding more drugs.

Toxoplasmosis
Normally a flu-like disease transmitted to humans through cats. In AIDS patients, it can cause encephalitis and can affect other internal organs.

Transfusion
To transfer blood, plasma or platelets from one person to another who needs it.

Tuberculosis
Disease spread through the air by bacteria. It usually affects the lungs and can be fatal even in non-AIDS patients. In AIDS patients, it can move beyond the lungs and infect other body systems.

Vaccine
A preventative medicine that contains parts of weakened diseases that are designed to stimulate the immune system and prepare it for an attack of the disease.

Viral load
A test that helps to determine how HIV is responding to treatment. It measures the amount of HIV in the blood.

Virus
A tiny piece of genetic material wrapped in a protein coat that needs a living cell to make copies of itself.

Wasting syndrome
Disease that affects AIDS patients where muscle and fat are lost. It will progress faster if a proper diet is not maintained.

Western Blot
The second test performed after the EIA/ ELISA for HIV to confirm the results. Electricity powers the movement of the sample through a thick gel. If HIV antibodies are present they get stuck in the gel.

Window

The time between when HIV enters your body and when the HIV infection can be measured with standard ELISA tests.

Help List

African Health Policy Network (AHPN)

Suite B5, New City Cloisters, 196 Old Street, London, EC1V 9FR
Tel: 020 7017 8910
info@ahpn.org
www.ahpn.org
The AHPN is designed to help Africans in the UK by fighting against the inequalities related to Africans with HIV.

AVERT

4 Brighton Road, Horsham, West Sussex, RH13 5BA, UK
info@avert.org
www.avert.org
Avert works to prevent HIV and AIDS worldwide by providing education, treatment, and care. It is an international organisation that is based in the UK.

Body and Soul

99 Rosebery Avenue, London, EC1R 4RE
Tel: 020 7923 6880
info@bodyandsoulcharity.org
www.bodyandsoulcharity.org
This is an organisation that targets children, young people and families living with HIV. Their goal is to take away the stress and isolation that come with a HIV diagnosis, and replace it with a healthy and brighter tomorrow.

British HIV Association (BHIVA)

Mediscript Ltd, 1 Mountview Court, 310 Friern Barnet Lane, London, N20 0LD, UK
Tel: 020 8369 5380
bhiva@bhiva.org
www.bhiva.org
BHIVA is an association that represents the professionals involved in HIV care. Although designed for professionals, the website provides access to HIV and AIDS research and up-to-date information.

British Red Cross

UK Office: 44 Moorfields, London, EC2Y 9AL
Tel: 0844 871 11 11
Text: 020 7562 2050
information@redcross.org.uk
www.redcross.org.uk
The British Red Cross provides HIV homecare programmes and educational information for people with HIV. They are a volunteer organisation designed to help anyone in crisis.

Derbyshire Positive Support

PO Box 124, Derby, DE1 9NZ
Tel: 01332 33 21 07
administration@dpsmail.org.uk
www.dpsweb.org
Derbyshire Positive Support offers support for people in Derbyshire who are HIV-positive as well as their friends and families. Aside from a variety of support services, they also offer information and education, HIV testing and respite care services.

HIV i-Base

4th Floor, 57 Great Suffolk Street, London, SE1 0BB
Tel: 020 7407 8488
admin@i-Base.org.uk
www.i-base.info
HIV i-Base is a HIV-positive lead activist group that provides information about treatment to HIV-positive people and healthcare professionals.

HIV Scotland

Suite 2, 27 Beaverhall Road, Edinburgh, EH7 4JE
Tel: 0131 558 3713
info@hivscotland.com
www.hivscotland.com
HIV Scotland was created to provide information and shape Scottish policy with relation to HIV-positive individuals.

Leicestershire AIDS Support Services (LASS)

The Michael Wood Centre, 53 Regent Road, Leicester, LE1 6YF
Tel: 0116 255 9995
reception@lass.org.uk
www.lass.org.uk
LASS provides support for people in Leicester and Rutland who are affected by AIDS. LASS also works to educate people to prevent the spread of HIV.

Metropolitan

The Welford Community Centre, 113 Chalkhill Road, Wembly, Middlesex, HA9 9FX
Tel: 020 3535 3535
www.metropolitan.org.uk
This company provides housing for people with HIV. They have offices in London, Nottingham, Derby, Sheffield and Cambridge.

National AIDS Manual (NAM)

77a Tradescant Road, London, SW8 1XJ
Tel: 020 3242 0820
info@nam.org.uk
www.aidsmap.com
NAM was founded to provide accurate and current information about AIDS.

National AIDS Trust (NAT)

New City Cloisters, 196 Old Street, London, EC1V 9FR
Tel: 020 7814 6767
info@nat.org.uk
www.nat.org.uk
NAT works to educate people and reform policies on AIDS and AIDS prevention.

NHS Direct

Tel: 0845 4647
www.nhsdirect.nhs.uk
You can use their website to find answers to your health questions or find providers. You can also contact them with medical questions.

Positively UK

345 City Road, London, EC1V 1LR
Tel: 020 7713 0444
info@positivelyuk.org
www.positivelyuk.org
Positively UK creates support networks for people who are HIV-positive and helps them manage treatment, cope with their diagnosis, and provides hardship support.

Sexual Health Line

Tel: 0800 56 71 23
The Sexual Health Line is a service that provides urgent assistance and advice on anything related to sexual health. It is available 24 hours a day, 7 days a week.

SHIELD

The Orchard Centre, 14-18 West Bar Green, Sheffield, S1 2DA
Tel: 0114 278 7916
www.shield.org.uk
SHIELD offers support and training services by developing an Individual
Support Plan that can include counselling, clinic outreach, and hardship
services.

Tagadere

c/o Nottingham CVS, 7 Mansfield Road, Nottingham, NG1 3FB
Tel: 07766 800 514
info@tagadere.org.uk
www.tagadere.org.uk
Tagadere (from the Old English word meaning 'together') is a self-help support
group for people living with HIV.

Terrence Higgins Trust (THT)

314-320 Gray's Inn Road, London, WC1X 8DP
Tel: 020 7812 1600
info@tht.gov.uk
www.tht.org.uk
Terrence Higgins was one of the first people in the UK to die of AIDS. After his
death, his friends and family founded this organisation, which was the first of
its kind in the UK. It was created to provide information to people with HIV on
housing, employments and benefits available to them. It also has an education
programme and provides clinical services. It has offices throughout the UK.

UK Community Advisory Board (UKCAB)

Memory Sachikonye, UKCAB, c/o HIV i-Base, 4th Floor, 57 Great Suffolk Street,
London, SE1 0BB
Tel: 020 7407 8488
memory.sachikonye@ukcab.net
www.ukcab.net
UK-CAB provides training on treatments to its members. Anyone who is an
HIV treatment advocate or HIV-positive may join and have access to the
information they provide.

Book List

Clinical Trials: A community guide to HIV research, March 2009
i-base. (Available from www.i-base.info)

Fluctuating symptoms of HIV, August 2011
National AIDS Trust. (Available from www.nat.org.uk)

Guidelines for Reporting HIV, 2010
National AIDS Trust. (Available from www.nat.org.uk)

HIV Public Knowledge and Attitudes, 2010
National AIDS Trust. (Available from www.nat.org.uk)

HIV Treatment as Prevention, 2011
National AIDS Trust. (Available from www.nat.org.uk)

Psychological Support for People Living with HIV, July 2010
National AIDS Trust. (Available from www.nat.org.uk)

Sexually Transmitted Infections: The Essential Guide, 2008
Need2Know books. (Available from www.need2knowbooks.co.uk)

References

Anonymous (2009) Quicksand: HIV/AIDS in Our Lives. Candlewick Press.

NAM aidsmap [Online] Available from http://www.aidsmap.com/First-UK-use-of-PrEP-for-couples-hoping-to-have-a-child/page/1765360/ [accessed 06 December 2012]

HIV and AIDS Treatment in the UK [Online] Available from http://www.avert.org/hiv-treatment-uk.htm [accessed 06 December 2012]

Bahl, A M, Hickson, J F (1995) Nutritional Care for HIV-Positive Persons: A Manual for Individuals and Their Caregivers. CRC Press.

Bardhan-Quallen, S (2005) Diseases and Disorders: AIDS. Thomson Gale.

Beck-Segue, C, Beck, C (2004) Deadly Diseases and Epidemics HIV/AIDS. Chelsea House Publishers.

Engle, J (2006) The Epidemic: A Global History of AIDS. Smithsonian Books Collins.

Farnan, R, Enriquez, M (2012) What Nurses Know…HIV/AIDS. Demos Health.

Judd, S J Ed. (2011) AIDS Sourcebook. Omnigraphics.

National AIDS Trust [Online] Available from www.nat.org.uk [accessed 19 November 2012]

Pacific AIDS Education and Training Center [Online] Available from http://www.aidsetc.org/aidsetc?page=etres-display&resource=etres-408 [accessed 19 November 2012]

Romeyn, M (1995) Nutrition and HIV: A New Model for Treatment. Jossey-Bass Publishers.

UK Study Shows How Better HIV Drugs Extend Lives [Online] Available from: http://www.reuters.com/article/2011/10/11/us-hiv-drugs-life-idUSTRE79A7I620111011 [accessed 13 December 2012]

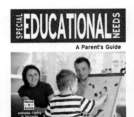  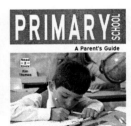  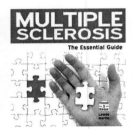